The books named „The power of women" contain many ideas that reflect a part of the immeasurable power of women.

The power of women in immeasurable and given by:

1. their special qualities

2. their abilities

3. their positive attitudes

4. their system of values

5. positive concepts about life

6. their life experiences

7. their aptitudes

8. their knowledge

9. their importance and necessity in the life of men, children, family and society.

10. their enormous and variety potential of doing positive, special acts for people, family and society.

11. etc…

Unfortunately, the power of women isn't known worldwide. Each country must do everything is necessary that women can achieve and use all of their power to do great facts to people, family and society.

The power of the women in the world is immeasurable and unfortunately this power is so rarely used for the good of humanity and society.

The ideas about women written in these books can help promote the women, their qualities, their power, to a better knowledge of the power of women and their special attu.

All the countries of the world, international organizations, Non-governmental organizations, Non-profit organizations, states institutions, and every man of the planet must contribute to developing the conditions that the women of the world can develop and use to the maximum of their special power in their own interest and in the interest of their families and human society.

The money invested in these books of mine and the others that follow it is worth it, and it is almost nothing comparing to the positive

The power of women

Book content:

effects that this book can have in your life, by applying the ideas to your life.

These volumes must be bought and used day by day, in order to development your personality and to the accomplish of all that you want.

These books contain lots of positive, optimist, creative, dynamic ideas, that push you to action, to thinking, things that are necessary your daily life and to accomplish your personal objectives.

Some of the ideas we might all know but when we need them mostly (in griefs, failures, when we want to have a solution to our problems), we don't remember them to help us when we need.

That's why it is necessary to have them organized in books and in need to read them.

Reading and analyzing the ideas in this book and applying them, we'll find solutions and ideas that will help us find:

I. To discover:

1. qualities

2. defects
3. capabilities
4. qualifications
5. some opportunities to succeed in life
6. feelings
7. what we do to be loved
8. how to love
9. how to realize and maintain a true mutual love
10. how to realize and maintain a happy marriage
11. mistakes, errors, wrong ideas
12. etc.

II. To prevent some:

1. divorces
2. mistakes
3. suspect
4. grief's
5. conflicts

6. accidents

7. failures

8. bankruptcy

9. etc.

III. To become more:

1. happy

2. loved

3. honored,

4. appreciated,

5. wanted,

6. optimistic,

7. good,

8. unselfish,

9. emotional,

10. altruists

11. stronger

12. efficient

13. organized

14. planners

15. active

16. honest

17. human

18. popular

19. famous

20. flexible

21. adaptable

22. understanding

23. prompt

24. etc.

IV. To get out of a state of:

1. despair

2. pessimism

3. passiveness

4. inactivity

5. inefficiency

6. inflexibility

7. crisis

8. inadaptability

9. etc.

V. To participate more actively to:

1. social life

2. political life

3. nonprofit organizations activities

4. etc

VI.   To participate more actively and efficiently in achieving true love and a happy marriage

VII.   To find more likely situations conducive to achieving and maintaining a happy marriage life

VIII.   To change our life for the better and to make it more beautiful

IX.   To multiply and increase the chances to find your life partner

X.   To raise and educate our children better so we can take better care of them

XI.   Find more and bigger chances to meet favorable situations to accomplish and maintain a happy marriage for life.

XII.   Change our life in good and make it better.

XIII. To multiply and increase the chances to find your life partner

XIV. To raise and educate our children better so we can take better care of them

I write and gather these thoughts, ideas in books, internet and other publications because these are useful to us every day and it is necessary to apply them to accomplish what we want, a better and beautiful life and prosperous.

These thoughts reflect a small part of what is good in reality and human relationships.

I wait to hear from you good news, good deeds that you have done influenced from what you have read from these books to make your life more beautiful, prosperous, happier and to be a positive example for others.

Each of us a become positive examples for others around us, participating to the creation of a better, prosperous and happier human society.

I'd be happy if one or more ideas read from these books helped you in a way or another and made you happier and prosperous.

I'm waiting to hear from you, your ideas and opinions, your joys and grief's and your suggestions for new book subjects and I also appeal to your participation of promoting on the internet and mass media of the ideas and the books I've written.

I invite you to e-mail me at my email address: agcornel@gmail.com.

Dear readers I wish you all health, happiness and achievement of all your wishes.

Best regards and respect,

Gheorghe Cornel Ardelean

981 Principal Street
Macea, Arad county
Zip Code 371210
Romania
Tel # (40)-0788-725-204
(40)-0788-725-913

Abilities

1. More of us would become happy and happier if they were more optimistic, if they knew their qualities, abilities, aptitudes and if they trusted themselves more.

2. As we have greater abilities to create more opportunities we do not get to situations of despair.

3. In life for as long as we live, it is necessary and useful to develop continuously, day by day, our creative skills and our creative abilities.

4. A leader does not like to be a leader with great success only if it has qualities and abilities to understand others as well.

5. Psychological discomfort greatly decreases the effectiveness of creative abilities.

6. Participating in social actions helps us develop our abilities to achieve and maintain a happy marriage.

7. Abilities help us become stronger.

8.   By developing new abilities, new attitudes and new qualities we will increase our chances very much to achieve personal goals.

9.   A man who can be trusted has the necessary abilities to achieve a true mature love.

10. The size and quality of experience is not only given by a life's duration but also by the intensity with which it has been lived, how much time was the work day by day, the area one has worked in, what one has worked, the qualities, and abilities, aptitudes and attitudes that man has, etc.

11. Experience helps us use and develop our abilities.

12. Solving problems through positive methods increases our abilities to achieve efficient co-developments.

13. Most of those who have the abilities to consciously choose also have trust in themselves.

14. People who have had successes know how to form and develop the necessary

abilities to achieve the successes they want to fulfill.

15. Those who know that discipline is the key to our dreams have the necessary abilities to maintain the desired efficient global co operations.

16. People who inspire trust have more abilities to achieve a more beautiful life.

17. Those who have not succeeded in achieving a happy marriage up to a certain date need, in order to succeed, they need to form and develop their abilities of creating strategies and ideas to find the right partner in life.

18. Women need to unite, to stay together and to cooperate in order to create a better world, because they have the abilities, the aptitudes, the qualities and the strength necessary to succeed.

19. The quality of learning how to learn helps us form the abilities we lead to achieve our personal goals.

20. Our abilities can be formed, developed, maintained and used through the

contribution of the formation, development, maintenance and usage of some cooperative behaviors.

21. Abilities can be formed, developed, maintained and used also through the contribution of the formation, development, maintenance and usage of balanced behaviors.

22. Abilities can be formed, developed, maintained and used through the contribution of the formation, development, maintenance and usage of the ability to react with understanding.

23. The abilities that do we need including those for achieving personal goals, can be formed, developed, maintained and used through the contribution of the formation, development, maintenance and usage of having a positive enterprising spirit.

24. Abilities can be formed, developed, maintained and used also through the contribution of the formation, development, maintenance and usage of behaviors that are imposed by the situation.

25.   Our abilities can be form, develop, maintain and use also through the contribution of the formation, development, maintenance and usage of the ability to relax.

Accomplishments

26.   We can contribute to the achievement of our greatest accomplishments also through the contribution of the formation, development, maintenance and usage of realistic behavior.

27.   We can contribute to the achievement of our greatest accomplishments also through the contribution of the formation, development, maintenance and usage of intellectual behavior.

28.   We can contribute to the achievement of our greatest accomplishments also through the contribution of the formation, development, maintenance and usage of diplomatic behavior.

29.   We can contribute to the achievement of our greatest accomplishments also through the contribution of the formation,

development, maintenance and usage of agreeable behavior.

30. We can contribute to the achievement of our greatest accomplishments also through the contribution of the formation, development, maintenance and usage of rigorous behavior.

31. We can contribute to the achievement of our greatest accomplishments also through the contribution of the formation, development, maintenance and usage of a behavior with scientific spirit.

32. We can contribute to the achievement of our greatest accomplishments also through the contribution of the formation, development, maintenance and usage of a behavior confident in success.

33. We can contribute to the achievement of our greatest accomplishments also through the contribution of the formation, development, maintenance and usage of continuous self-education behavior.

34. We can contribute to the achievement of our greatest accomplishments also through the contribution of the formation,

development, maintenance and usage of bold behavior.

35.   We can contribute to the achievement of our greatest accomplishments also through the contribution of the formation, development, maintenance and usage of creative behavior.

36.   We can contribute to the achievement of our greatest accomplishments also through the contribution of the formation, development, maintenance and usage of flexible behavior.

37.   We can contribute to the achievement of our greatest accomplishments also through the contribution of the formation, development, maintenance and usage of sturdy behavior.

38.   We can contribute to the achievement of our greatest accomplishments also through the contribution of the formation, development, maintenance and usage of self-confident behavior.

39.   We can contribute to the achievement of our greatest accomplishments also through the contribution of the formation,

development, maintenance and usage of popular behavior.

40. We can contribute to the achievement of our greatest accomplishments also through the contribution of the formation, development, maintenance and usage of continuous self-economizing behavior.

41. We can contribute to the achievement of our greatest accomplishments also through the contribution of the formation, development, maintenance and usage of kind behavior.

42. We can contribute to the achievement of our greatest accomplishments also through the contribution of the formation, development, maintenance and usage of active behavior.

43. We can contribute to the achievement of our greatest accomplishments also through the contribution of the formation, development, maintenance and usage of pleased behavior.

44. We can contribute to the achievement of our greatest accomplishments also through the contribution of the formation,

development, maintenance and usage of efficient behavior.

45. We can contribute to the achievement of our greatest accomplishments also through the contribution of the formation, development, maintenance and usage of stimulating behavior.

46. We can contribute to the achievement of our greatest accomplishments also through the contribution of the formation, development, maintenance and usage of selfless behavior.

47. We can contribute to the achievement of our greatest accomplishments also through the contribution of the formation, development, maintenance and usage of audacious behavior.

48. We can contribute to the achievement of our greatest accomplishments also through the contribution of the formation, development, maintenance and usage of patient behavior.

49. We can contribute to the achievement of our greatest accomplishments also through the contribution of the formation,

development, maintenance and usage of decisive behavior.

50.   We can contribute to the achievement of our greatest accomplishments also through the contribution of the formation, development, maintenance and usage of leadership behavior.

Active

51.   People who are full of energy and active have a higher capacity to achieve personal goals.

52.   People who are full of energy and active have more and greater chances to achieve true friendships.

53.   Those who are skeptical are less active.

54.   Usually, those who are optimistic are more active.

55.   People who are full of energy and active have more and greater chances to meet more favorable situations.

56.   People who are full of energy and active have higher chances to succeed in life.

57. People who are full of energy and active have a larger contribution in achieving the greater good.

58. People who are full of energy and active are engines of progress in all areas of activity.

59. People who are full of energy and active have more and greater chances to achieve themselves.

60. Those who are a lot more active, who work daily accumulate more experience than those who are lazy and less active.

61. Our life at the moment offers a great number of people, more and greater chances of having a happy life, but unfortunately many are too passive, too inactive and wait for luck to run them over.

62. Luck runs into the one who is active, dynamic and industrious.

63. People who are full of life and active have more possibilities to find the right partner for life.

64. People who are full of life and active have a high capacity to test their efficiency.

65. People with the sense of discipline participate more actively to global humanization.

66. People who are full of life and active have a greater capacity to achieve outstanding performances.

67. People who are full of life and active have more and greater chances to achieve a happier life.

68. People who are full of life and active have greater and more chances to achieve a more beautiful life.

69. People who are full of life and active have more chances to achieve their desired future.

70. Self delusion stops us from being active in solving a problem or problems that delude us.

71. People who have a high level of energy are very active.

72. A man full of energy and active must be promoted.

73. People who are full of life and active have a greater ability to contribute to the humanization of society.

74. People who are full of life and active have much more and greater chances to achieve their own happiness.

75. People who are full of life and active have much more and greater chances to achieve efficient co operations.

76. AGC mediations help us become more active.

77. In order to follow and transform our personal goals into reality, it is necessary to also form, develop, maintain and use our active behavior.

78. The necessary qualities in achieving personal goals can be formed, developed, maintained and used also through the contribution of the formation, development, maintenance and usage of active behavior.

79. Continuous self-control helps us become active.

80. Hope helps us become active.

81. We can become stronger and we can not allow ourselves to be influenced by the world also through the contribution of the formation, development, maintenance and usage of active behavior.

82. Problems cannot be solved by the ideas that created them but also through the contribution of the formation, development, maintenance and usage of active behavior.

83. The radical transformation for the better of our life can be achieved also through the formation, development, maintenance and usage of active behavior.

84. Responsibility helps us become active.

85. Communication helps us become active.

86. Rather than lamenting that we do not have successes it is more useful to also form, develop, maintain and use active behavior.

87. Pessimism can be removed and replaced with optimism also through the contribution of the formation, development, maintenance and usage of active behavior.

88. Our future can be projected and achieved also through the contribution of the formation, development, maintenance and usage of active behavior.

89. Continuous self-motivation helps us become active.

90. Self-imposed discipline helps us become active.

91. Our own happiness can be achieved and maintained also through the contribution of the formation, development, maintenance and usage of active behavior.

92. In order to prevent failures it is necessary to also form, develop, maintain and use active behavior.

93. Stress can be prevented also through the formation, development, maintenance and usage of active behavior.

94. Release from our self-imposed restrictions can be made also through the contribution of the formation, development, maintenance and usage of active behavior.

95. In order to escape poverty it is necessary to also form, develop, maintain and use active behavior.

96. In achieving our successes a contribution is also brought by the formation, development, maintenance and usage of active behavior.

Appreciate

97. The activity of voluntarism must be encouraged and appreciated at its just value.

98. Kindness makes us appreciated.

99. Those who recognize other people's actions are people who are appreciated by their collaborators

100. Reliability makes us be much more appreciated.

101. Self control must always be promoted, sustained, appreciated, respected and rewarded.

102. Work must always be promoted, sustained, appreciated, respected and rewarded.

103. Those with the sense of responsibility must be appreciated, promoted, supported and rewarded.

104. A very sociable man is much appreciated.

105. Those willing to try new ways must be appreciated.

106. A man who is full of energy and active must be appreciated.

107. Careful people must be appreciated.

108. Prejudices must not be appreciated.

109. Independence must always be promoted, appreciated, respected and rewarded.

110. The sense of responsibility needs to be appreciated, promoted, supported and respected.

111. He who is very conscious is much appreciated.

112. Those who are capable of self control in stressing situations must be appreciated, promoted, sustained and rewarded.

113. Those with a greater resistance to stress must be appreciated.

114. Men who have wives who earn more than they do need to appreciate them very much.

115. Honor must be promoted, supported, appreciated, respected and rewarded.

116. Courage must always be promoted, supported, appreciated, respected and rewarded.

117. Polite people are respected, appreciated and esteemed.

118. Communicative people are appreciated, respected, esteemed and rewarded.

119. Magnanimity must be respected, appreciated, esteemed and rewarded.

120. Efficient human communication must be appreciated, promoted, sustained and rewarded.

121. Those who are enthusiastic must be appreciated, promoted, supported and rewarded.

122. Those who are very conscious need to be promoted, appreciated, supported and rewarded.

123. People who inspire trust must be appreciated.

124. People with the sense of discipline must be appreciated.

125. Those with the sense of objectivity must be appreciated.

126. The state of certainty must be appreciated.

127. Magnanimity is a quality that makes us very appreciated by people.

128. Constructive thinking must be appreciated.

129. The majority of those with the ability to react with understanding are appreciated.

130. People who are not careful with others must not be appreciated.

131. Those who only solve problems through constructive methods must be appreciated.

132. Solving problems through positive methods must be appreciated.

133. People who have success appreciate their success.

134. People who take positive decisions must be appreciated.

135. People who are not careful with others are not appreciated.

136. The need to succeed must be appreciated.

137. The majority of those who have the ability to react with understanding must be appreciated.

138. People who know how to motivate must be appreciated.

139. Those who live their life passionately and not at random must be appreciated.

140. The majority of those involved in many new projects must be appreciated.

141. The inner beauty of a woman is more and more appreciated by man.

142. Man needs to appreciate inner beauty in women as a priority.

143. Sometimes we sacrifice ourselves for many people but few of them appreciate the gesture.

144. A man with many qualities is highly appreciated.

145. Kindness makes us be appreciated.

146. The inner beauty of a woman is more and more appreciated by more men.

147. The more a man has more qualities the more appreciated he will be.

148. A man who is willing at any time to help someone is highly appreciated and loved by people.

149. Responsibility must always be promoted, supported, appreciated, respected and rewarded.

Beautiful

150. Life is too beautiful for a part of it to be spent in prison in order to satisfy our greed.

151. We can make our life more beautiful if we are realistic.

152. We can make our life more beautiful if we are organized.

153. Sociable individuals have much greater opportunities to achieve a beautiful life.

154. We can make life a lot more beautiful if we only act with an effective positive behavior.

155. Compliance with principles helps us achieve a beautiful life.

156. Life is more beautiful when you have successes.

157. A responsible behavior helps us have more opportunities to achieve a beautiful life.

158. If we use the Internet to the maximum in solving the problems and needs that we have, it would make our life much easier,

more enjoyable, more beautiful. Good luck. If you have not connected yet, connect because it is worth it. Good luck.

159. We can make our life more beautiful if we plan our action very well.

160. We can make our life more beautiful if we are always careful.

161. We can make our life more beautiful if we are disciplined.

162. We can make our life beautiful if we are fair.

163. We can make our life beautiful if we are enthusiastic.

164. Life is too beautiful to spend part of its freedom in prison to satisfy the desire of luxury.

165. The harmony between family members makes life more beautiful.

166. Life is too beautiful for a part of it to be spent in prison for negligence or lack of attention.

167. Regardless of how we live, it is not worth it to be alone which makes our life less beautiful.

168. Life has been given to us not to fight with it but to live it beautifully.

169. Hopes make our life more beautiful.

170. Activism makes our life more beautiful.

171. We can create a more beautiful life if we are less stressed.

172. We can create a more beautiful life if we are optimistic.

173. Life is too beautiful for us to spend a significant part of it in prison.

174. Co-development makes our life more beautiful.

175. Consensus helps us prevent and eliminate many obstacles in front of us on the road to achieving a more beautiful life.

176. We can make our life more beautiful if we are not stressed.

177. We can make our life more beautiful and if we have more qualities.

178. We can make our life more beautiful and if we have more skills.

179. We can make our life more beautiful and if we have creative attitudes.

180. Life is too beautiful to be spent a part of it in prison in order to satisfy greed.

181. We can make life a lot more beautiful if we only have effective positive behaviors.

182. Life is more beautiful when we have successes.

183. A responsible behavior helps us have more chances to make our life more beautiful.

184. If we use the Internet to the maximum in solving problems and needs that we have, it makes our life easier, more enjoyable, more beautiful. Good luck. If you are not connected, connect as it is worth it for all reasons and purposes. Good luck.

185. A positive experience makes our life more beautiful.

186. Good humor makes our life more beautiful.

187. True friendship makes our life more beautiful.

188. Life would be much more beautiful without vices.

189. Meditations help us make a more beautiful life.

190. Most of the times social relations make life more beautiful.

191. Friendships help us make a more beautiful life.

192. The desire to lead a beautiful life must be owned by each of us.

193. For people in the world's states there are much more chances and possibilities to obtain a more beautiful life with the help of technology.

194. Life is much more beautiful when we have hopes.

195. We can make life more beautiful if we have an appropriate education for us to achieve it.

196. The efficient management of our time helps us and increases our chances to achieve a beautiful life.

197. We need to use our life experience to achieve a more beautiful life.

198. Day by day the chances for more people to achieve a more beautiful life grow.

199. Credibility helps us a lot to make our life more beautiful.

200. Life can be more beautiful if we do not hate.

201. Life can be more beautiful if we do not hold grudges.

202. Humanist global thinking can create more possibilities for a higher number of people to achieve a more beautiful life.

203. People who produce useful ideas have bigger chances to achieve a more beautiful life.

204. A man who is emotionally stable has more chances to achieve a more beautiful life

205. A man capable of self control in stressing situations has the power and great chances to achieve a more beautiful life.

206. A man who is realistic in interpersonal relations has more chances and a higher potential to achieve a more beautiful life.

207. A man sure of himself has great chances to achieve a more beautiful life.

208. Self-imposed discipline helps us and contributes a lot in achieving a more beautiful life.

Beauty

209. A woman with an inner beauty does much good to mankind.

210. A woman with an inner beauty must be idolized.

211. A woman with an inner beauty has great chances to achieve a happy marriage.

212. A woman with an inner beauty has more chances to achieve a long lasting marriage.

213. A woman with an inner beauty has more chances to maintain a happy marriage.

214. A woman with an inner beauty has more chances to maintain a long lasting marriage.

215. A woman with an inner beauty has the chances to maintain true love.

216. A woman with an inner beauty has great chances to promote her husband.

217. Unfortunately today, on the 25th of March, 2009 women with inner beauty are not appreciated by society to their just value.

218. The inner beauty of the woman must be appreciated by the man.

219. The inner beauty of the woman must be appreciated by society.

220. The inner beauty of the woman must be appreciated by women.

221. The inner beauty of women must be supported.

222. The inner beauty of women must be encouraged.

223. The inner beauty of women must be promoted.

224. The inner beauty of women must be protected.

225. Inner beauty must be rewarded.

226. The inner beauty of women must be maintained.

227. The inner beauty of the woman prevents many troubles.

Calm

228. Obtaining more and greater successes can be achieved also through the contribution of the formation, development, maintenance, usage of a calm behavior.

229. The radical transformation for the better of our life can be achieved also through the formation, development, maintenance and usage of calm behavior.

230. The necessary qualities in achieving personal goals can be formed, developed, maintained and used also through the contribution of the formation, development, maintenance and usage of calm behavior.

231. Our happiness depends a lot also on the formation, development, maintenance and usage of calm behavior.

232. In order to rise up once again for the first time for the who knows what time it is necessary to also form, develop, maintain and use calm behavior.

233. Stress can be prevented also through the formation, development, maintenance and usage of calm behavior.

234. The obstacles that prevent us from achieving our personal goals can be surpassed also through the contribution of the formation, development, maintenance and usage of calm behavior.

235. Self-imposed discipline helps us become calm.

236. Release from our self-imposed restrictions can be made also through the contribution of the formation, development, maintenance and usage of calm behavior.

237. Rather than lamenting that we do not have successes it is more useful to also form, develop, maintain and use calm behavior.

238. Our future can be projected and achieved also through the contribution of the formation, development, maintenance and usage of calm behavior.

239. Continuous self-motivation helps us become calm.

240. In order to escape poverty it is necessary to also form, develop, maintain and use calm behavior.

241. We can form, develop and maintain the state of being ourselves also through the contribution of the formation, development, maintenance and usage of a calm behavior.

242. We can prevent some failures also through the contribution of the formation, development, maintenance and usage of calm behavior.

243. The limits of achievement imposed by ourselves in our mind at a given moment can be overcome or eliminated also through the contribution of the formation, development, maintenance and usage of calm behavior.

Careful

244. People who are not careful with others have smaller chances of achieving their personal goals.

245. People who are not careful with others do not usually care about the greater good.

246. Young people need and must be very careful not to make the same mistakes as their predecessors by taking from their experience only positive models and experience

247. Careful men have fewer failures.

248. People who are careful must be promoted.

249. People who are careful have greater and more chances to achieve personal goals.

250. By listening very carefully to what people who have had successes say and by taking from them the ideas that are useful we can form, develop, maintain and use a positive live conception.

251. By listening very carefully to what people who have had successes say and by taking from them the ideas that are useful

to us we can form, develop, maintain and use the ideas that help us motivate ourselves.

252. People who are not careful with others are not rewarded.

253. People who are not careful with others have difficulties in participating in achieving efficient co operations.

254. People who are not careful with others achieve a happier life a lot harder.

255. People who are not careful with others are not supported.

256. People who are not careful with others have a small contribution or none at all to global humanization.

257. People who are not careful with others come more believable a lot harder.

258. People who are not careful with others are not promoted.

259. People who are not careful what others have many failures.

260. People who are not careful with others are rejected.

261. People who are not careful with others achieve their desired future a lot farther.

262. Those who have high objectives in life are mostly careful with others.

263. By the listening very carefully to what people who have had successes say and by taking from them the ideas that are useful to us we can form, develop, maintain and use a constructive conception of life.

264. By listening very carefully to what people who have had successes say and by taking some ideas that are useful from them we can form, develop, maintain and use the ability to create cooperation in a team.

265. By listening very carefully to what people who have had successes say and by taking some ideas that are useful from them we can form, develop, maintain and use a long term conception of life.

266.   By listening very carefully to what people who have had successes say and by taking the ideas that are useful from them we can form, develop, maintain and use the sense of commitment in everything we do.

267.   By listening very carefully to what people who have had successes say and by taking the ideas that are useful from them we can form, develop, maintain and use a social conception of life.

268.   By this inning very carefully to what people who have had successes say and by taking from them the ad as that are useful, we can form, develop, maintain and use the ability to succeed in our personal life.

269.   By listening very carefully to what people who have had successes say and by taking useful ideas from them we can form, develop, maintain and use an efficient conception of life.

270.   By listening very carefully to what people who have had successes say and by taking useful ideas from them we can form, develop, maintain and use the ability

to maintain the necessary efficient co-developments.

Charitable

271. We can form, develop and maintain the state of being ourselves also through the contribution of the formation, development, maintenance and usage of a charitable behavior.

272. The limits of achievement imposed by ourselves in our mind at a given moment can be overcome or eliminated also through the contribution of the formation, development, maintenance and usage of charitable behavior.

273. Our own happiness can be achieved and maintained also through the contribution of the formation, development, maintenance and usage of charitable behavior.

274. Our future can be projected and achieved also through the contribution of the formation, development, maintenance and usage of charitable behavior.

275. Aspiring towards a more meaningful life can also be achieved through the

formation, development, maintenance and usage of charitable behavior.

276. In order to escape poverty it is necessary to also form, develop, maintain and use charitable behavior.

277. Stress can be prevented also through the formation, development, maintenance and usage of charitable behavior.

278. In achieving our successes a contribution is also brought by the formation, development, maintenance and usage of charitable behavior.

279. Positive experience can be achieved also through the contribution of the formation, development, maintenance and usage of charitable behavior.

280. The necessary qualities in achieving personal goals can be formed, developed, maintained and used also through the contribution of the formation, development, maintenance and usage of charitable behavior.

281. In order to prevent failures it is necessary to also form, develop, maintain and use charitable behavior.

282. Continuous self-motivation helps us become charitable.

283. The radical transformation for the better of our life can be achieved also through the formation, development, maintenance and usage of charitable behavior.

Charming

284. In order to prevent failures it is necessary to also form, develop, maintain and use charming behavior.

285. In achieving our successes a contribution is also brought by the formation, development, maintenance and usage of charming behavior.

286. In order to prevent not achieving our personal goals, it is necessary to also form, develop, maintain and use our charming behavior.

287. We can contribute to the achievement of our greatest accomplishments also

through the contribution of the formation, development, maintenance and usage of charming behavior.

288. The self efficient use of our time helps us become charming.

289. Responsibility helps us become charming.

290. We can prevent some failures also through the contribution of the formation, development, maintenance and usage of charming behavior.

291. In order to escape poverty it is necessary to also form, develop, maintain and use charming behavior.

292. Wisdom helps us become charming.

293. We can overcome the difficulties that we must overcome also through the help of the formation, development, maintenance and usage of charming behavior.

294. Creativity helps us become charming.

295. The solutions to the problems we have or that we want to solve can be found also through the contribution of the formation,

development, maintenance and usage of charming behavior.

296. We can become stronger and we can not allow ourselves to be influenced by the world also through the contribution of the formation, development, maintenance and usage of charming behavior.

Cheerful

297. The limits of achievement imposed by ourselves in our mind at a given moment can be overcome or eliminated also through the contribution of the formation, development, maintenance and usage of cheerful behavior.

298. Release from our self-imposed restrictions can be made also through the contribution of the formation, development, maintenance and usage of cheerful behavior.

299. Wisdom helps us become cheerful.

300. The solutions to the problems we have or that we want to solve can be found also through the contribution of the formation,

development, maintenance and usage of cheerful behavior.

301.   Continuous self-motivation helps us become cheerful.

302.   Responsibility helps us become cheerful.

303.   Will helps us become cheerful.

304.   Rather than lamenting that we do not have successes it is more useful to also form, develop, maintain and use cheerful behavior.

305.   Acting efficiently helps us become cheerful.

306.   The necessary qualities in achieving personal goals can be formed, developed, maintained and used also through the contribution of the formation, development, maintenance and usage of cheerful behavior.

307.   We can prevent some failures also through the contribution of the formation, development, maintenance and usage of cheerful behavior.

308. Aspiring towards a more meaningful life can also be achieved through the formation, development, maintenance and usage of cheerful behavior.

309. Our own happiness can be achieved and maintained also through the contribution of the formation, development, maintenance and usage of cheerful behavior.

310. Continuous self perfection helps us become cheerful.

311. In order to prevent failures it is necessary to also form, develop, maintain and use cheerful behavior.

312. The obstacles that prevent us from achieving our personal goals can be surpassed also through the contribution of the formation, development, maintenance and usage of cheerful behavior.

313. Some mistakes can be prevented also through the contribution of the formation, development, maintenance and usage of cheerful behavior.

314. Optimism helps us become cheerful.

315. Positive experience can be achieved also through the contribution of the formation, development, maintenance and usage of cheerful behavior.

Cheerishing

316. Cherishing oneself helps us achieve more performances.

317. Cherishing oneself helps us achieve more efficient co operations.

318. Cherishing oneself helps us achieve more pleasant surprises.

319. Cherishing oneself helps us achieve more true friendships.

320. Cherishing oneself helps us achieve a true love.

321. Cherishing oneself helps us become trained.

322. A great capacity of cherishing oneself helps us achieve more pleasant surprises.

323. Cherishing oneself helps us become voluble.

324. A great capacity of cherishing oneself helps us become loved.

325. A great capacity of cherishing oneself helps us become optimistic.

326. Cherishing oneself helps us become tenacious.

327. Cherishing oneself helps us become capable.

328. A great capacity of cherishing oneself helps us become tolerant.

329. Cherishing oneself helps us become respectful.

330. Cherishing oneself helps us become joyful.

331. Rather than lamenting that we do not have successes it is more useful to also form, develop, maintain and use self-cherishing behavior.

332. A great capacity of cherishing oneself must be supported.

333. Cherishing oneself helps us become friendly.

334. Cherishing oneself helps us become loyal.

335. A great capacity of cherishing oneself helps us become more cautious.

336. A great capacity of cherishing oneself must be rewarded.

337. A great capacity of cherishing oneself helps us maintain our way of being loved.

338. A great capacity of cherishing oneself helps us achieve more favorable chances.

339. The radical transformation for the better of our life can be achieved also through the formation, development, maintenance and usage of self cherishing behavior.

340. A great capacity of cherishing oneself must be a model.

341. A great capacity of cherishing oneself helps us become more optimistic.

342. Cherishing oneself helps us become consequent.

343. Cherishing oneself helps us become sure of ourselves.

344. A great capacity of cherishing oneself helps us become more practical.

345. Cherishing oneself helps us become stimulating.

346. Cherishing oneself helps us become spontaneous.

347. Cherishing oneself helps us become energetic.

348. Cherishing oneself helps us become idealistic.

349. Cherishing oneself helps us become convincing.

350. A great capacity of cherishing oneself helps us become more loving.

351. A great capacity of cherishing oneself helps us maintain our way of being loving.

352. A great capacity of cherishing oneself must be formed.

353. We can form, develop and maintain the state of being ourselves also through the contribution of the formation, development, maintenance and usage of a self-cherishing behavior.

Communicative

354. Communicative women have more chances of becoming what they want to.

355. Optimistic women are more communicative.

356. Open minded people are more communicative.

357. Communicative people more quickly make true friends.

358. Communicative people achieve a lot easier true friendships.

359. Communicative people earn the trust of others a lot faster.

360. Communicative people are more open-minded.

361. Communicative people get into contact with people a lot faster.

362. Rather than lamenting that we do not have successes it is more useful to also form, develop, maintain and use communicative behavior.

363. In order to prevent failures it is necessary to also form, develop, maintain and use communicative behavior.

364. In order to rise up once again for the first time for the who knows what time it is necessary to also form, develop, maintain and use communicative behavior.

365. We can form, develop and maintain the state of being ourselves also through the contribution of the formation, development, maintenance and usage of a communicative behavior.

366. Stress can be prevented also through the formation, development, maintenance and usage of communicative behavior.

367. Continuously making ourselves efficient helps us become more communicative.

368. Obtaining more and greater successes can be achieved also through the contribution of the formation, development, maintenance, usage of a communicative behavior.

369. In order to escape poverty it is necessary to also form, develop, maintain and use communicative behavior.

Constructive

370. Constructive thinking helps us achieve only constructive behaviors.

371. We can broaden our horizon more or less also through the contribution of the formation, development, maintenance and usage of constructive thinking.

372. Those who do not think enough need to form, develop, maintain and use constructive thinking.

373. Problems cannot be solved by the ideas of that created them but also through the contribution of the formation, development, maintenance and usage of constructive behaviors.

374. Emancipation from self imposed restrictions can be made through the formation, development and maintenance of a great ability to solve problems through constructive methods.

375. Forming wrong ideas can be prevented also through the formation, development, maintenance and usage of constructive thinking.

376. In order to change our life it is necessary to form, develop, maintain and use constructive behaviors.

377. Doubts can be removed using constructive thinking.

378. Finding the meaning of our lives can be achieved through also using constructive ideas.

379. Solutions to the problems we have can be found through the usage of constructive life conceptions.

380. The force of our ideas can be augmented also through the contribution of the formation, development, maintenance and usage of constructive life conceptions.

381. The development of our thinking can be achieved also through the formation, development, maintenance and usage of constructive ideas.

382. The state of psychical discomfort can be removed through the formation, development and maintenance of constructive thinking.

383. We can overcome difficulties through the formation, development and maintenance of constructive thinking.

384. Despair can be eliminated through the contribution of a constructive life conception.

385. In order to pursue and transform positive objectives into reality it is necessary to form and develop constructive thinking.

386. In order to pursue and transform positive objectives into reality it is necessary to form and develop a constructive conception of life.

387. The state of psychical discomfort can be removed through the formation, development and maintenance of a constructive conception of life.

388. In order to pursue and transform positive objectives into reality it is necessary to

form, develop, maintain and use constructive thinking.

389. In order to rise up once again for the first time, for the second time, for the who knows what time, it is necessary to form, develop, maintain and use constructive thinking.

390. We can distinguish right from wrong better and faster also through the contribution of formation, development, maintenance and usage of constructive thinking.

391. Abilities can be formed, developed, maintained and used also through the contribution of the formation, development, maintenance and usage of a constructive life conception.

392. Despair can be eliminated also through the contribution of formation, development, maintenance and usage of constructive thinking.

393. Our remaining in ignorance can be eliminated also through the contribution of the formation, development, maintenance and usage of a constructive conception of life.

394. By listening very carefully to what people who have had successes say and by taking useful ideas from them we can form, develop, maintain and use a constructive life conception.

395. Obstacles that stop us from achieving our personal goals can be overcome also through the contribution of the formation, development, maintenance and usage of constructive thinking.

396. Emancipation from restrictions can be made through the formation, development and maintenance of a constructive conception of life.

397. Doubts can be eliminated through the formation, development, maintenance and usage of a constructive life conception.

398. Our transformation for the better of our life can be achieved through the formation, development, maintenance and usage of a constructive conception of life.

399. Finding the meaning of life can be achieved by using constructive ideas.

400. Forming wrong ideas about what is happening to us can be prevented by using a constructive thinking.

401. Emancipation from restrictions can be made through the formation, development and support of constructive thinking.

402. Finding the meaning of our lives can be achieved also through the contribution of the formation, development, maintenance and usage of a constructive life conception.

403. Constructive actions make us more credible.

404. Constructive thinking makes us believable.

405. Constructive ideas help us a lot to to achieve a happy life.

406. Successes in life can also be achieved thanks to constructive thinking.

407. Our chances of becoming happy increase if we form a constructive thinking.

Convincing

408. Communication helps us become convincing.

409. A great capacity of being convincing must be a model.

410. A great capacity of being convincing helps us maintain our efficiency.

411. A great capacity of being convincing helps us achieve more personal goals.

412. We can prevent some failures also through the contribution of the formation, development, maintenance and usage of convincing behavior.

413. The limits of achievement imposed by ourselves in our mind at a given moment can be overcome or eliminated also through the contribution of the formation, development, maintenance and usage of convincing behavior.

414. A great capacity of being convincing helps us become more productive.

415. We can form, develop and maintain the state of being ourselves also through the

contribution of the formation, development, maintenance and usage of a convincing behavior.

416. A great capacity of being convincing helps us become optimistic.

417. Hopes can be created also through the contribution of the formation, development, maintenance and usage of convincing behavior.

418. A great capacity of being convincing helps us achieve more records.

419. A great capacity of being convincing helps us become more efficient.

420. Problems cannot be solved by the ideas that created them but also through the contribution of the formation, development, maintenance and usage of convincing behavior.

421. A great capacity of being convincing helps us maintain our way of being loving.

422. Obtaining more and greater successes can be achieved also through the contribution of the formation, development,

maintenance, usage of a convincing behavior.

423. In order to prevent not achieving our personal goals, it is necessary to also form, develop, maintain and use our convincing behavior.

424. The necessary qualities in achieving personal goals can be formed, developed, maintained and used also through the contribution of the formation, development, maintenance and usage of convincing behavior.

425. A great capacity of being convincing helps us become more optimistic.

426. A great capacity of being convincing helps us maintain our enthusiasm.

427. Confidence in ourselves helps us become convincing.

428. A great capacity of being convincing helps us become more tolerant.

429. Positive experience can be achieved also through the contribution of the formation,

development, maintenance and usage of convincing behavior.

430. A great capacity of being convincing must be encouraged.

431. Our resistance to changing for the better can be overcome also through the contribution of the formation, development, maintenance and usage of convincing behavior.

432. A great capacity of being convincing must be imitated.

433. A great capacity of being convincing helps us achieve more pleasant surprises.

434. Aspiring towards a more meaningful life can also be achieved through the formation, development, maintenance and usage of convincing behavior.

435. Pessimism can be removed and replaced with optimism also through the contribution of the formation, development, maintenance and usage of convincing behavior.

436. A great capacity of being convincing must be formed.

437. In order to stand up once again for the first time or for the who knows what time, it is necessary to also form, develop, maintain and use convincing behavior.

438. Our future can be projected and achieved also through the contribution of the formation, development, maintenance and usage of convincing behavior.

439. A great capacity of being convincing helps us become more practical.

440. Rather than lamenting that we do not have successes it is more useful to also form, develop, maintain and use convincing behavior.

441. A great capacity of being convincing must be supported.

442. Hope helps us become convincing.

443. A great capacity of being convincing helps us achieve more favorable chances.

444. A great capacity of being convincing helps us maintain our humanity.

445. A great capacity of being convincing helps us become tolerant.

446. A great capacity of being convincing helps us become more humane.

447. A great capacity of being convincing helps us become more cautious.

448. We can become stronger and we can not allow ourselves to be influenced by the world also through the contribution of the formation, development, maintenance and usage of convincing behavior.

Correct

449. Persons with humane social behavior need to have a correct thinking.

450. Prejudices can be prevented through correct and complete information.

451. Correct relations with coworkers contribute lot in achieving more and greater successes.

452. Correct relations with coworkers help us become more efficient.

453. Correct relations with coworkers help us achieve more harmonious social relations.

454. The sense of responsibility contributes a lot in achieving some correct social relations.

455. Problems cannot be solved by the ideas that created them but through other ideas and through the contribution of formation, development, maintenance, and the usage of correct thinking.

456. In order to take correct decisions it is necessary to form, develop, maintain and use the ability to be responsible.

457. Problems cannot be solved by the ideas of that created them but also through the contribution of the formation, development, maintenance and usage of correct thinking.

458. In order to trace and transform our personal goals into reality it is necessary that we form and develop correct thinking.

459. Forming wrong ideas can be prevented also through the formation, development,

maintenance and usage of correct thinking.

460. Preventing the formation of doubts can be achieved also through the formation, development, maintenance and usage of a correct life conception.

461. Preventing the formation of doubt can be achieved also through the formation, development, maintenance and usage of correct thinking.

462. Those who have high objectives in life mostly have a correct thinking.

463. Persons who have not succeeded in building a happy marriage up to a certain date, in order to succeed they need to form and develop a correct thinking.

464. People who know how to take quality decisions also have a correct thinking.

465. Most of those who know how to prevent possible mistakes also have a correct thinking.

466. Those who have the obligation to choose correctly must not be underestimated.

467. Preventing stress can be achieved also through the contribution of the formation, development, maintenance and usage of correct behaviors.

468. Emancipation from self imposed restrictions can be done also through the contribution of the formation, development, maintenance and usage of correct thinking.

469. Rather than lamenting that we do not have successes it is better to form, develop and maintain correct thinking.

470. The desire to make others happy can be achieved through the contribution of the formation, development, maintenance and usage of correct thinking.

471. We can replace wrong ideas with correct ideas also through the contribution of the formation, development, maintenance and usage of constructive ideas.

472. Correct thinking can be formed, developed, maintained and used also through the contribution of the formation, development, maintenance and usage of correct ideas.

473. Preventing stress can be achieved also through the contribution of the formation, development, maintenance and usage of a correct behavior.

474. In order to pursue and transform our personal goals into reality we need to form and develop correct thinking.

Courage

475. States need to encourage, push and reward innovation not be against it.

476. Courage must always be promoted, supported, appreciated, respected and rewarded.

477. A man with courage has a high potential to achieve personal goals.

478. Efficient co-developments must be encouraged.

479. States need to encourage, stimulate, and reward the more effective use of society's resources both by people and companies for the good of people and society.

480. People who have had successes have a lot of courage.

481. States need to motivate and encourage more the production of ideas.

482. States need and must support, impel, encourage, reward the formation and development of inner beauty in women.

483. States need and must support, impel, encourage and reward the formation and development of man's inner beauty.

484. A man with courage achieves efficient co-developments also.

485. A man with courage makes many friends.

486. A man who has courage has great chances to succeed in life.

487. A man with courage has a great potential to achieve more and greater successes.

488. A man with courage has great chances to achieve efficient co operations.

489. Rather than being discouraged it is a lot better to search for solutions in solving the problems that we have.

490. Courage can be created, developed, maintained and used through the

contribution of the formation, development, maintenance and usage of an objective behavior.

491. In order to trace and transform our personal goals into reality it is necessary that we form and develop the ability to form courage when we are discouraged.

492. Those who have high objectives in life mostly have much courage.

493. The uncertainties of incomes discourage people.

494. In order to pursue and transform our objectives into reality it is necessary to form, develop, maintain and use the ability to be courageous.

495. In order to pursue and transform our personal goals into reality we need to form and develop the ability to be courageous and discouraged.

496. Courage can be created, developed, increased, maintained and used also through the contribution of the formation, development, maintenance and usage of experimental behaviors.

497. Courage can be formed, developed, maintained and used also through the contribution of the formation, development, maintenance and usage of corresponding behaviors imposed by the situation.

498. Courage can be created, developed, increased, maintained and used also through the contribution of the formation, development, maintenance and usage of an objective behavior.

499. Courage can be formed also by assuming risks.

500. In order to pursue and transform positive objectives into reality it is necessary to form, develop, maintain and use the ability to be courageous.

501. Courage can be developed through the formation, development, maintenance and usage of responsible behaviors.

502. The encouragement of positive behaviors is a vital necessity.

503. The encouragement of positive thinking is a vital necessity.

504. Positive ambition must always be encouraged.

505. Oprimistic attitude must be encouraged.

506. Optimistic attitude must be encouraged in children when they're very young.

507. Hopes must be encouraged.

508. Communication between friends must be encouraged.

509. Abuse must be discouraged by the law.

510. True friends encourage each other.

511. True friendships must be encouraged.

512. Creativity must be encouraged.

513. Positive deeds must be encouraged.

514. Women must be encouraged continuously to perfect themselves.

Creativity

515. Creativity helps us achieve more true friendships.

516. Creativity helps us achieve a true love.

517. Creativity helps us become perfectionists.

518. Creativity helps us become audacious.

519. A great capacity of increasing creativity helps us become tolerant.

520. A great capacity of increasing creativity helps us maintain our way of being practical.

521. Creativity helps us become self controlled.

522. A great capacity of increasing creativity helps us become optimistic.

523. Creativity helps us become rigorous.

524. Creativity helps us become animated.

525. A great capacity of increasing creativity helps us become happy.

526. Creativity helps us become energetic.

527. A great capacity of increasing creativity helps us become understanding.

528. A great capacity of increasing creativity helps us maintain our way of being loving.

529. Creativity helps us become cheerful.

530. A great capacity of increasing creativity must be encouraged.

531. A great capacity of increasing creativity helps us become wise.

532. Creativity helps us become spontaneous.

533. A great capacity of increasing creativity helps us achieve more personal goals.

534. A great capacity of increasing creativity helps us become more productive.

535. Creativity helps us become spiritual.

536. Creativity helps us become persevering.

537. Creativity helps us become analytic.

538. Creativity helps us become leaders.

539. Creativity helps us become voluble.

540. A great capacity of increasing creativity helps us maintain our way of being cautious.

541. A great capacity of increasing creativity helps us become more humane.

542. Creativity helps us become rulers.

543. A great capacity of increasing creativity helps us become more preventive.

544. Creativity helps us become respectful.

545. Creativity helps us become sturdy.

546. Creativity helps us become mannered.

547. Creativity helps us become cultivated.

548. A great capacity of increasing creativity helps us become loving.

549. Creativity helps us become good listeners.

550. A great capacity of increasing creativity must be appreciated.

551. Creativity helps us become penetrating.

552. Creativity helps us become joyful.

553. Creativity helps us become peacemakers.

554. Creativity helps us become convincing.

555. Creativity helps us become reserved.

556. A great capacity of increasing creativity helps us become more cautious.

557. A great capacity of increasing creativity helps us become happier.

558. A great capacity of increasing creativity helps us become more optimistic.

559. Creativity helps us become pleasant.

560. A great capacity of increasing creativity helps us maintain our happiness.

561. A great capacity of increasing creativity must be developed.

562. A great capacity of increasing creativity helps us become more tolerant.

563. A great capacity of increasing creativity helps us achieve more efficient co operations.

564. Creativity helps us become strong.

565. A great capacity of increasing creativity helps us maintain our way of being liked.

566. A great capacity of increasing creativity helps us become loved.

567. Creativity helps us become adaptable.

568. A great capacity of increasing creativity helps us maintain our wisdom.

569. Creativity helps us become confident.

570. A great capacity of increasing creativity helps us become efficient.

571. A great capacity of increasing creativity must be supported.

Credibility

572. The sense of fairness increases our credibility.

573. The sense of credibility helps us become more credible.

574. A positive enterprising spirit increases our credibility.

575. Credibility many times brings us luck.

576. People who are resistant to stress have a greater credibility.

577. A non hostile but aggressive behavior helps us increase our credibility.

578. Concentrating our energies increases our credibility.

579. Sometimes the lack of common sense enormously reduces the credibility of the ones who do not have common sense.

580. The sense of organization increases our credibility.

581. The sense of objectivity increases the credibility of the person who has it.

582. Those who know that discipline is one of the keys of dreams increased their credibility.

583. Efficient people in positive actions have more chances of increasing their credibility.

584. Those who willingly expand their positive experience increase their credibility.

585. Those who control circumstances increase their credibility.

586. Constructive thinking increases our credibility.

587. Long term thinking increases our credibility.

588. A positive conception of life increases our credibility.

589. Those who discover unique ways to work efficiently for a better life increase their credibility.

590. Solving problems through positive methods increases our credibility.

591. Moral values continuously increase our credibility.

Daring

592. Problems cannot be solved by the ideas that created them but also through the contribution of the formation, development, maintenance and usage of daring behavior.

593. Continuous self perfection helps us become daring.

594. Our resistance to changing for the better can be overcome also through the contribution of the formation, development, maintenance and usage of daring behavior.

595. Pessimism can be removed and replaced with optimism also through the contribution of the formation, development, maintenance and usage of daring behavior.

596. In order to escape poverty it is necessary to also form, develop, maintain and use daring behavior.

597. The necessary qualities in achieving personal goals can be formed, developed, maintained and used also through the contribution of the formation, development, maintenance and usage of daring behavior.

598. In achieving our successes a contribution is also brought by the formation, development, maintenance and usage of daring behavior.

599. Continuous self-control helps us become daring.

600. Creativity helps us become daring.

601. Hopes can be created also through the contribution of the formation, development,

maintenance and usage of daring behavior.

602. Some mistakes can be prevented also through the contribution of the formation, development, maintenance and usage of daring behavior.

603. Will helps us become daring.

604. Communication helps us become daring.

605. We can become stronger and we can not allow ourselves to be influenced by the world also through the contribution of the formation, development, maintenance and usage of daring behavior.

606. Hope helps us become daring.

Diplomatic

607. The necessary qualities in achieving personal goals can be formed, developed, maintained and used also through the contribution of the formation, development, maintenance and usage of diplomatic behavior.

608. Our future can be projected and achieved also through the contribution of the

formation, development, maintenance and usage of diplomatic behavior.

609. Cherishing oneself helps us become diplomatic.

610. In order to rise up once again for the first time for the who knows what time it is necessary to also form, develop, maintain and use diplomatic behavior.

611. Creativity helps us become diplomatic.

612. Positive experience can be achieved also through the contribution of the formation, development, maintenance and usage of diplomatic behavior.

613. Acting efficiently helps us become diplomatic.

614. Continuous self-control helps us become diplomatic.

615. The self efficient use of our time helps us become diplomatic.

616. Hope helps us become diplomatic.

617. Rather than lamenting that we do not have successes it is more useful to also form,

develop, maintain and use diplomatic behavior.

618. Wisdom helps us become diplomatic.

619. Will helps us become diplomatic.

620. Hopes can be created also through the contribution of the formation, development, maintenance and usage of diplomatic behavior.

621. Self-imposed discipline helps us become diplomatic.

622. Pessimism can be removed and replaced with optimism also through the contribution of the formation, development, maintenance and usage of diplomatic behavior.

623. The limits of achievement imposed by ourselves in our mind at a given moment can be overcome or eliminated also through the contribution of the formation, development, maintenance and usage of diplomatic behavior.

624. Optimism helps us become diplomatic.

625. Our happiness depends a lot also on the formation, development, maintenance and usage of diplomatic behavior.

626. We can overcome the difficulties that we must overcome also through the help of the formation, development, maintenance and usage of diplomatic behavior.

627. Aspiring towards a more meaningful life can also be achieved through the formation, development, maintenance and usage of diplomatic behavior.

628. We can become stronger and we can not allow ourselves to be influenced by the world also through the contribution of the formation, development, maintenance and usage of diplomatic behavior.

629. Our own happiness can be achieved and maintained also through the contribution of the formation, development, maintenance and usage of diplomatic behavior.

630. Communication helps us become diplomatic.

631. Continuously making ourselves efficient helps us become diplomatic.

Disciplined

632. A disciplined man has a greater potential to achieve a happy life.

633. A disciplined man has a greater potential to achieve more and greater outstanding performances.

634. A disciplined man has a great potential to increase his efficiency.

635. Those who are disciplined succeed more easily.

636. Those who are disciplined have more chances to obtain happiness.

637. Those who are disciplined have more chances to achieve efficient co operations.

638. Those who are disciplined have more chances to find their partner for life.

639. Those who are remarkably gifted are disciplined.

640. People who can prevent possible mistakes are disciplined.

641. Problems cannot be solved by the ideas that created them but also through the

contribution of the formation, development, maintenance and usage of Self-imposed disciplined behaviors.

642. Successes are achieved if we are disciplined.

Docile

643. Continuously making ourselves efficient helps us become docile.

644. Pessimism can be removed and replaced with optimism also through the contribution of the formation, development, maintenance and usage of docile behavior.

645. We can prevent some failures also through the contribution of the formation, development, maintenance and usage of docile behavior.

646. Our resistance to changing for the better can be overcome also through the contribution of the formation, development, maintenance and usage of docile behavior.

647. Creativity helps us become docile.

648. Wisdom helps us become docile.

649. In order to prevent failures it is necessary to also form, develop, maintain and use docile behavior.

650. Problems cannot be solved by the ideas that created them but also through the contribution of the formation, development, maintenance and usage of docile behavior.

651. Rather than lamenting that we do not have successes it is more useful to also form, develop, maintain and use docile behavior.

652. The force of our ideas can be augmented also through the contribution of the formation, development, maintenance and usage of docile behavior.

653. Will helps us become docile.

654. In order to rise up once again for the first time for the who knows what time it is necessary to also form, develop, maintain and use docile behavior.

655. We can become stronger and we can not allow ourselves to be influenced by the

world also through the contribution of the formation, development, maintenance and usage of docile behavior.

656. The radical transformation for the better of our life can be achieved also through the formation, development, maintenance and usage of docile behavior.

657. Continuous self-motivation helps us become docile.

658. Hope helps us become docile.

659. Stress can be prevented also through the formation, development, maintenance and usage of docile behavior.

660. Our happiness depends a lot also on the formation, development, maintenance and usage of docile behavior.

Eager

661. The radical transformation for the better of our life can be achieved also through the formation, development, maintenance and usage of a behavior of being eager for knowledge.

662. Some mistakes can be prevented also through the contribution of the formation, development, maintenance and usage of a behavior eager for knowledge.

663. We can contribute to the achievement of our greatest accomplishments also through the contribution of the formation, development, maintenance and usage of a behavior eager for knowledge.

664. We can form, develop and maintain the state of being ourselves also through the contribution of the formation, development, maintenance and usage of a behavior eager for knowledge.

665. Self-imposed discipline helps us become eager for knowledge.

666. Our future can be projected and achieved also through the contribution of the formation, development, maintenance and usage of a behavior of being eager for knowledge.

667. Continuous self-motivation helps us become eager for knowledge.

668. We can prevent some failures also through the contribution of the formation, development, maintenance and usage of a behavior of being eager for knowledge.

669. We can prevent the falling apart of a happy marriage also through the contribution of the formation, development, maintenance and usage of a behavior eager for knowledge.

670. In order to rise up once again for the first time for the who knows what time it is necessary to also form, develop, maintain and use a behavior of being eager for knowledge.

671. In achieving our successes a contribution is also brought by the formation, development, maintenance and usage of a behavior of being eager for knowledge.

672. Positive experience can be achieved also through the contribution of the formation, development, maintenance and usage of a behavior eager for knowledge.

673. Stress can be prevented also through the formation, development, maintenance and

usage of a behavior of being eager for knowledge.

674. Aspiring towards a more meaningful life can also be achieved through the formation, development, maintenance and usage of a behavior of being eager for knowledge.

675. Our resistance to changing for the better can be overcome also through the contribution of the formation, development, maintenance and usage of a behavior eager for knowledge.

Education

676. Inadequate education reduces the number and quality of opportunities to find favorable situations.

677. Improper education reduces efficient co operations.

678. Improper education reduces our possibilities of achieving true friendships.

679. A proper education stops the state of despair.

680. A proper education prevents many failures.

681. The more we have a proper education suited for our needs, the more chances we have of not reaching the situation of despair.

682. Self education helps us form an optimal morale.

683. An optimal morale can be formed through a proper diet, education, intellectual exercises, perseverance, will, physical exercises, etc.

684. Good humor can be maintained through a balanced life, a proper diet, education, intellectual exercises, psychical balance, perseverance, women, physical exercises, a value system in which we believe in and that we respect, positive activities, dynamism, social relations, friends, mature love, a happy marriage, etc.

685. The level of situations and present technologies, the experience, the education, the resources of all kind allow and impose the development of harmonious global co-development

thinking and the achieving of many global programs and projects.

686. Improper education reduces a lot our chances of having success.

687. Improper education reduces our efficiency.

688. Psychical balance can be obtained through education, will, perseverance.

689. Positive thinking can be maintained through a proper diet, education, intellectual exercise, perseverance, experience, will, physical exercises, etc.

690. Many acts of domestic violence can be prevented through education in schools, universities, on the Internet, in the media, etc.

691. Permanently, continuously, day by day, for as long as we live it is necessary to have the personal goal to increasingly support education and self-education for children to achieve a harmonious personality.

692. Inadequate education is directly or indirectly the cause of most crimes.

693. Inadequate education reduces the efficiency that we could achieve.

694. Inadequate education gives a smaller quality and number of opportunities we have to achieve efficient co-development.

695. We can make life more beautiful if we have an appropriate education for us to achieve it.

696. A psychological balance can be maintain once achieved through the proper nutrition of the person concerned, through education, intellectual work, perseverance, experience, willingness, physical exercises, etc.

697. Positive thinking can be achieved if you do not have it through the proper nutrition of the person concerned, through education, intellectual work, perseverance, experience, willingness, physical exercises, etc.

698. Good mood can be achieved if the person concerned has adequate nourishment, it can be achieved through education, intellectual work, perseverance, willpower, exercise, a value system that we believe in

and that we respect, business dynamism, social relationships, friends, mature love and a happy marriage.

699. Fatigue can be prevented through the proper nutrition of the person concerned, through education, positive behavior, balanced life, intellectual exercises, perseverance, willpower, exercise, a value system that we believe in and that we respect, business dynamism, social relations, friends, mature love, a happy marriage, adequate rest when necessary, proper sleep, entertainment, etc..

700. Inadequate education is a major cause of many crimes.

701. By making a proper education states can prevent many crimes.

702. States need to take the immediate necessary measures to provide a proper education efficiency to be able to prevent many crimes by this method, which consists in carrying out an effective appropriate education for people who do not want to commit crimes.

703. Effective state investments in an education that is corresponding and against the disobedience of laws is worth the efforts, because if it is of a good quality, very effective and very attentively created it produces multiple and various effects paying back the positive investments made and an additional huge profit if analyzed in terms of financial efficiency of the investment.

704. States should be especially concerned to achieve a proper education effective from all points of view to respond to real the needs of education of the people and society and to effectively satisfy both their needs.

705. An appropriate efficient education meant to meet the needs of people and society is particularly important for people and for society, but unfortunately, even in 2007, many states do not have a proper effective education to meet the requirements and needs of people and of society concerning education.

706. Advanced education is an engine of our self-achievement.

707. Advanced education contributes a lot to global humanization.

708. An advanced education greatly facilitates the achievement of social relations.

709. An advanced education helps a lot in achieving true love.

Efficient

710. The power of continuous efficient organization helps us achieve more performances.

711. The willpower of not allowing ourselves to be stopped helps us achieve more efficient co operations.

712. Knowing our profession helps us achieve more efficient co operations.

713. Knowing what is necessary for us to know helps us achieve more efficient co operations.

714. Our everyday effective actions help us achieve more efficient co operations.

715. Preventing the inefficient use of the resources of informatics helps us achieve more personal goals.

716. Useful ideas help us achieve more efficient co operations.

717. Rising from more failures helps us achieve more efficient co operations.

718. The desire to be better helps us achieve more efficient co operations.

719. The great capacity of taking efficient decisions helps us achieve more efficient co operations.

720. Preventing the inefficient use of financial resources helps us achieve much good luck.

721. The passion of achieving personal goals helps us achieve more efficient co operations.

722. Preventing the inefficient use of the resources of informatics helps us achieve more efficient co operations.

723. Permanent concentration on our personal objectives helps us achieve more efficient co operations.

724. Openness towards new efficient actions helps us achieve much good luck.

Encouraging

725. A great capacity of encouraging people helps us maintain our tolerance.

726. A great capacity of encouraging people helps us become efficient.

727. A great capacity of encouraging people must be rewarded.

728. A great capacity of encouraging people must be used.

729. A great capacity of encouraging people helps us maintain our productivity.

730. A great capacity of encouraging people helps us achieve more records.

731. A great capacity of encouraging people helps us become loved.

732. A great capacity of encouraging people helps us maintain our happiness.

733. A great capacity of encouraging people helps us achieve more pleasant surprises.

734. A great capacity of encouraging people helps us become wise.

735. A great capacity of encouraging people helps us become more cautious.

736. A great capacity of encouraging people helps us become happy.

737. A great capacity of encouraging people helps us become optimistic.

738. A great capacity of encouraging people helps us become more productive.

739. A great capacity of encouraging people helps us become understanding.

740. A great capacity of encouraging people helps us maintain our way of being liked.

741. A great capacity of encouraging people must be imitated.

742. A great capacity of encouraging people must be a model.

743. A great capacity of encouraging people helps us achieve more personal goals.

744. A great capacity of encouraging people helps us maintain our way of being loved.

745. A great capacity of encouraging people helps us become humane.

746. A great capacity of encouraging people helps us become more loved.

747. A great capacity of encouraging people helps us become enthusiastic.

748. A great capacity of encouraging people must be encouraged.

749. A great capacity of encouraging people helps us maintain our enthusiasm.

750. A great capacity of encouraging people helps us become more understanding.

751. A great capacity of encouraging people must be formed.

752. A great capacity of encouraging people helps us achieve more efficient co operations.

753. A great capacity of encouraging people must be maintained.

754. A great capacity of encouraging people helps us become more loving.

755. A great capacity of encouraging people helps us become productive.

756. A great capacity of encouraging people helps us maintain our way of being loving.

757. A great capacity of encouraging people helps us become practical.

758. A great capacity of encouraging people helps us become more tolerant.

759. A great capacity of encouraging people helps us maintain our way of being understanding.

760. A great capacity of encouraging people helps us maintain our wisdom.

761. A great capacity of encouraging people helps us become more efficient.

762. A great capacity of encouraging people helps us achieve more favorable situations.

Energy

763. People who are full of energy and active are engines of progress in all areas of activity.

764. People who are full of energy and active have more and greater chances to achieve themselves.

765. People who have successes mostly have a high level of energy.

766. There are many women and many men who can form and have happy marriages, but they do not find each other although they could. They do too little and spend too little time in finding each other; they consume their time and energy for things that are less important.

767. Young men have an enormous amount of energy that can contribute greatly with enormous immediate positive effects to solving all local or general problems of mankind.

768. People who have a high level of energy are very active.

769. Those who do not have hopes, in order to create hopes for the future need to connect with people who have a high level of energy.

770. Those who have high objectives in life are mostly full of energy.

771. The self-control of our flaws helps us a lot to prevent the waste of energy.

Enterprising

772. In order to trace and transform our personal objectives into reality it is necessary to form, develop, maintain and use a positive enterprising sense.

773. A positive enterprising spirit increases our ability to achieve efficient co operations.

774. An enterprising spirit can be really achieved through a larger exchange of information.

775. A positive enterprising spirit increases the ability to succeed in life.

776. A positive enterprising spirit makes us be supported.

777. A positive enterprising spirit creates greater possibilities to create a more beautiful life.

778. Those who have no hopes, in order to create their hopes in the future need to connect with people who have a positive enterprising spirit.

779. A positive enterprising spirit increases our ability to maintain a happy marriage.

780. A positive enterprising spirit increases our trust in the future.

781. A positive enterprising spirit increases our ability to achieve efficient co-developments.

782. A positive enterprising spirit positively increases our capacity to prevent possible failures in life.

783. Those who do not have hopes, in order to create hopes for the future need to connect with those with an efficient enterprising spirit.

784. An enterprising spirit increases our possibilities of achieving more social relations.

785. An enterprising spirit must be appreciated.

786. An enterprising spirit helps us become even more performing.

787. People who know how to take quality decisions are enterprising.

788. People who want success must have an enterprising spirit.

789. A positive enterprising spirit increases our ability to achieve true friendships.

790. A positive enterprising spirit increases our capacity to achieve a happy marriage.

791. Enterprising people in positive actions must be promoted.

792. Those who do not have hopes, in order to create hopes for the future, need to develop their efficient enterprising spirit.

Enthusiasm

793. Those who are enthusiastic contribute through their enthusiasm to maintaining our health.

794. Those who are enthusiastic through their enthusiasm have greater chances to meet more favorable situations.

795. Optimism increases our enthusiasm.

796. Those who are enthusiastic have high chances to achieve a happy marriage with their enthusiasm.

797. Enthusiasm increases and maintains our perseverance.

798. An enthusiasm increases our power.

799. Optimism maintains our enthusiasm.

800. Personal goals also create enthusiasm.

801. Those who are enthusiastic become more credible through their enthusiasm.

802. The state of annoyance reduces our enthusiasm a lot.

803. The state of restlessness reduces a lot our enthusiasm.

804. The state of fatigue reduces a lot our enthusiasm.

805. Optimism creates enthusiasm.

806. True love increases our enthusiasm.

807. By orienting towards a future world we increase our enthusiasm.

808. In order to follow and transform our personal goals into reality, it is necessary to also form, develop, maintain and use our enthusiasm.

809. A great capacity of anticipating helps us maintain our enthusiasm.

810. A great capacity of using available ideas helps us maintain our enthusiasm.

811. A great capacity of using a value system helps us maintain our enthusiasm.

812. A great capacity of being honest with oneself helps us maintain our enthusiasm.

813. A great capacity of using abilities helps us maintain our enthusiasm.

814. A great capacity of establishing high personal goals helps us maintain our enthusiasm.

815. A great capacity of using available resources helps us maintain our enthusiasm.

816. A great capacity of using qualities helps us maintain our enthusiasm.

817. A great capacity of persevering until finding creative solutions helps us maintain our enthusiasm.

818. A great capacity of doing what is best helps us maintain our enthusiasm.

819. A great capacity of establishing great personal goals helps us maintain our enthusiasm.

820. A great capacity of not letting others lead one's life helps us maintain our enthusiasm.

821. A great capacity of using available knowledge helps us maintain our enthusiasm.

Facing

822.   A great capacity of facing one's own life helps us become enthusiastic.

823.   A great capacity of facing one's own life must be supported.

824.   A great capacity of facing one's own life helps us become cautious.

825.   A great capacity of facing one's own life helps us become happier.

826.   A great capacity of facing one's own life must be rewarded.

827.   A great capacity of facing one's own life helps us become loved.

828.   A great capacity of facing one's own life helps us become more tolerant.

829.   A great capacity of facing one's own life helps us maintain our way of being understanding.

830.   A great capacity of facing one's own life helps us become more preventive.

831.   A great capacity of facing one's own life must be used.

832. A great capacity of facing one's own life helps us become more pleasant.

833. A great capacity of facing one's own life helps us maintain our efficiency.

834. A great capacity of facing one's own life helps us maintain our way of being practical.

835. A great capacity of facing one's own life helps us achieve more favorable situations.

836. A great capacity of facing one's own life helps us maintain our way of being cautious.

837. A great capacity of facing one's own life helps us maintain our happiness.

838. A great capacity of facing one's own life helps us achieve more true friendships.

839. A great capacity of facing one's own life must be maintained.

Failures

840. If we lack perseverance in life we get a lot of failures.

841. If we have a short-term thinking we will have many failures in life.

842. Absurd actions lead to failures.

843. The man who approaches and is used to address problems simultaneously from different points of view is much likely to have great potential to prevent many failures.

844. The man who operates continuously, day by day, to become more efficient is more likely, has more chances and a growing potential to prevent many failures.

845. The sense of organization contributes a lot to preventing many failures.

846. Those willing to try new ways have greater chances to achieve fewer failures.

847. Preventive actions help us to prevent much more possible failures.

848. If we are inefficient we will have many failures.

849. If we have defects, we do not have the qualities necessary to do what we need to do and we have failures.

850. In everything we do we need to document ourselves on how to best prevent failures.

851. Inefficient behaviors surely lead us to failures.

852. Continuous failures unite people to help them get through their depression.

853. Failures should never defeat our optimism.

854. If we disturb others we will have many failures in life.

855. If we are undocumented in what we do we will have many failures.

856. If we do not plan actions we will have many failures.

857. Those who are unruly have many failures in life.

858. If you have had failures you should not worry but continue what you have started if it is positive.

859. Failure or failures should not discourage us.

860. Often, if we had failures, we can learn much more from them than from

successes, but this should not justify our failures, but look for the causes of failures and take preventive measures to stop our future failures.

861. Failures must never immobilize us.

862. If you are disorderly you will have many failures.

863. If we are distracted we will have many failures in life.

864. If we are indisciplined we will have many failures in life.

865. If we are unfair we will have many failures in life.

866. Conceit has led to many failures for the conceited one.

867. Conceit creates many failures.

868. Prejudices are often the causes of many failures.

869. Immorality is a factor of many failures.

870. If we are stressed we have more failures in life.

871. If we are inexperienced in what we do we can have failures.

872. If you are lazy you will have many failures in life.

873. If we are pessimistic it is possible to have more failures than if we would be optimistic.

874. If we have flaws and we do not have the qualities needed in what we do we will have failures.

875. In everything we do we need to document better to prevent failures.

876. Those who are disorderly have a lot of failures in life.

877. A failure or failures should not discourage us.

878. You have to use failures as a stepping-stone to other successes.

879. Often, if we have a failure we can learn more from it than from a success, but this does not have to justify failure, we must look for the causes of that failure and take preventive measures to stop other failures.

880. Negative behaviors lead us to failures.

881. We are each responsible for our own failures.

882. A proper education prevents many failures.

883. Failures make us more cautious.

884. Failures create pessimism.

885. Discipline in everything we do helps us prevent certain failures.

886. It is illegal to try to make others responsible for our own failures.

887. Fatigue creates failures.

888. Calm people in any situation have greater chances to prevent more failures.

889. The man who is cooperative in activities has greater chances to prevent more failures.

890. Concentrating our energies helps us prevent many failures.

891. A man sure of himself has great possibilities of preventing many failures.

892. Those who know how to choose the way that fits them best have the possibility to prevent many failures.

893. People who are used to carrying out the activities they had started have a high capacity to prevent many failures.

894. Those who are enthusiastic through their enthusiasm have a higher capacity to prevent many failures.

895. Those who hardly keep an interpersonal relation have fewer failures.

Fairness

896. Fairness sometimes brings us to luck.

897. We can overcome the difficulties that we need to overcome also through the formation, development and maintenance of the sense of fairness in everything we do.

898. Forming wrong ideas can be prevented also through the formation, development, maintenance and usage of the sense of fairness.

899. Those who have high objectives in life mostly have the sense of fairness.

900. People with human social behaviors need to have the sense of fairness.

901. People who know how to prevent possible mistakes mostly have the sense of fairness.

902. Persons who have the ability to react with understanding also have the sense of fairness.

903. People who have had successes mostly have the sense of fairness as well.

904. Those who do not have hopes, in order to create hopes for the future, they need to get themselves involved in relations with people who have the sense of fairness.

905. In order to pursue and transform our objectives into reality it is necessary to form, develop, maintain and use the sense of fairness as well.

906. The state of psychical discomfort can be removed also through the formation,

development and maintenance of the sense of fairness.

907. In achieving successes a contribution is brought by the formation, development, maintenance and usage of the ability to face the lack of fairness.

908. We can overcome difficulties that we must overcome also through the formation, development and maintenance the sense of fairness in everything we do.

909. The desire to make others happy can be achieved through the contribution of the formation, development, and maintenance of fairness.

910. The state of psychical discomfort can be removed also through the formation, development and maintenance of the sense of fairness in everything we do.

911. In order to change it is necessary to form, develop, maintain and use the sense of fairness.

912. Forming wrong ideas can be prevented through the contribution of the formation,

development, maintenance and usage of the sense of fairness.

913. In order to pursue and transform positive objectives into reality it is necessary to form, develop, maintain and use the sense of fairness.

914. We can overcome difficulties through the formation, development and maintenance of the sense of fairness.

915. In order to pursue and transform positive objectives into reality it is necessary to form and develop the sense of fairness.

916. Emancipation from restrictions can be made through the formation, development and support of the sense of fairness.

917. Fairness between friends contributes to maintaining that friendship.

918. Fairness helps us more easily make friends.

919. Fairness helps us maintain true friendships.

920. Fairness demands fairness.

921. Fairness must be repaid with fairness.

922. True friendships assume fairness between friends.

923. Friends must reward each other's fairness with fairness.

Faith

924. The faithfulness of collaborators helps us achieve more personal goals.

925. The faithfulness of collaborators helps us achieve more performances.

926. The faithfulness of collaborators helps us achieve more efficient co operations.

927. The faithfulness of collaborators helps us achieve more pleasant surprises.

928. The faithfulness of collaborators helps us achieve more favorable chances.

929. The faithfulness of collaborators helps us achieve more favorable situations.

930. The faithfulness of collaborators helps us achieve more records.

931. The faithfulness of collaborators helps us achieve more successes.

932. The faithfulness of collaborators helps us achieve much good luck.

Family

933. Spouses need and must be respectful to one another to maintain harmony, understanding and happiness in the family.

934. When respect disappears between spouses in a family, disputes arise, conflicts, arguments, mistrust and ultimately it is very likely in many families for divorce to occur.

935. Each of the spouses need to always be calculated in family relations in order to prevent arguments, conflicts, misunderstandings etc..

936. Alcoholism is a primary cause of many divorces; it has negative effects on the family.

937. In a family, its members may not joke with what could negatively affect the harmony,

understanding and happiness of the family and sometimes with what could lead to divorce.

938. Sometimes, in a few cases from certain offenses, a family can reach a divorce.

939. For a family to prevent divorce, it is necessary to do everything they can to preserve the marriage, harmony, understanding, etc..

940. Spouses need to comply with those rules in the family that make them have good relations and harmony in the family.

941. Abstention is partly, the art of knowing how to abstain within the family, in the relations with the other, with children, other family members (parents, parents-in-law, grandparents, brothers, brothers-in law, etc.), it is a part of the wisdom of each of the spouses, that is useful for us to develop.

942. Forethought is a quality that is required of each spouse in the family. Only with forethought a husband and wife can avoid many potential trouble, failures, conflicts, etc. in marriage.

943. Consensus helps us maintain harmony in the family.

944. Our ingenuity helps us create and maintain a happy family.

945. Those who have had a negative thinking in certain situations had many troubles, failures, conflicts in the family, some came to divorce, and they have achieved little success too.

Feelings

946. People who have had successes mostly have envious feelings.

947. Our happiness depends on the power to control our feelings.

948. When you are in love you have more intense feelings.

949. When you are in love you have different feelings.

950. Feelings must be expressed.

951. Feelings must be appreciated.

952. Feelings must be rewarded with feelings.

953. Spouses must reveal their feelings mutually.

954. When spouses reveal their feelings mutually they contributes a lot to maintaining a happy marriage.

955. When lovers reveal their feelings mutually they contribute a lot to maintaining true love.

956. When friends reveal their feelings mutually they contribute a lot to maintaining a true friendship.

957. When people reveal their feelings mutually they contribute a lot to maintaining inter-human relations.

958. AGC mediations help us discover feelings.

959. By developing their inner beauty, women also develop their feelings.

Flexibility

960. People who have had successes have the sense of flexibility.

961. Forming wrong ideas can be prevented also through the formation, development, maintenance and usage of flexibility.

962. Emancipation from restrictions can be made through the formation, development and maintenance of the sense of flexibility.

963. The limits we have set can be overcome by the formation, development, maintenance and usage of the sense of flexibility.

964. In order to transform positive objectives into reality it is necessary to form, develop, maintain and use the sense of flexibility.

965. Flexibility increases our chances of achieving more successes.

966. Flexibility increases our chances of achieving more objectives.

Friendly

967. In order to escape poverty it is necessary to also form, develop, maintain and use friendly behavior.

968. A great capacity of being friendly helps us become more pleasant.

969. Creativity helps us become friendly.

970. Hope helps us become friendly.

971. A great capacity of being friendly helps us become happy.

972. Will helps us become friendly.

973. A great capacity of being friendly must be used.

974. A great capacity of being friendly must be maintained.

975. Our own happiness can be achieved and maintained also through the contribution of the formation, development, maintenance and usage of friendly behavior.

976. Continuous self perfection helps us become friendly.

977. In order to rise up once again for the first time for the who knows what time it is necessary to also form, develop, maintain and use friendly behavior.

978. The self efficient use of our time helps us become friendly.

979. A great capacity of being friendly helps us become more cautious.

980. A great capacity of being friendly helps us become more practical.

981. A great capacity of being friendly helps us become more enthusiastic.

982. A great capacity of being friendly helps us become optimistic.

983. A great capacity of being friendly helps us maintain our productivity.

984. A great capacity of being friendly must be formed.

985. A great capacity of being friendly helps us become more preventive.

Funny

986. Continuous self-motivation helps us become funny.

987. Positive experience can be achieved also through the contribution of the formation, development, maintenance and usage of funny behavior.

988. The self efficient use of our time helps us become funny.

989. Responsibility helps us become funny.

990. We can prevent the falling apart of a happy marriage also through the contribution of the formation, development, maintenance and usage of funny behavior.

991. In order to escape poverty it is necessary to also form, develop, maintain and use funny behavior.

992. Our resistance to changing for the better can be overcome also through the contribution of the formation, development, maintenance and usage of funny behavior.

993. Continuously making ourselves efficient helps us become funny.

994. Obtaining more and greater successes can be achieved also through the contribution of the formation, development, maintenance, usage of a funny behavior.

995. Our own happiness can be achieved and maintained also through the contribution of

the formation, development, maintenance and usage of funny behavior.

996. We can become stronger and we can not allow ourselves to be influenced by the world also through the contribution of the formation, development, maintenance and usage of funny behavior.

997. The solutions to the problems we have or that we want to solve can be found also through the contribution of the formation, development, maintenance and usage of funny behavior.

998. The obstacles that prevent us from achieving our personal goals can be surpassed also through the contribution of the formation, development, maintenance and usage of funny behavior.

999. In order to rise up once again for the first time for the who knows what time it is necessary to also form, develop, maintain and use funny behavior.

1000. Rather than lamenting that we do not have successes it is more useful to also form, develop, maintain and use funny behavior.

1001. Self-imposed discipline helps us become funny.

1002. In order to prevent failures it is necessary to also form, develop, maintain and use funny behavior.

1003. Hope helps us become funny.

Giving

1004. Friendships sometimes make us more forgiving.

1005. Forgiving is a noble behavior.

1006. Forgiving is a positive behavior.

1007. Forgiving is a wise behavior.

1008. Never giving up helps us achieve more pleasant surprises.

1009. Never giving up helps us achieve more true friendships.

1010. Never giving up helps us achieve more successes.

1011. Never giving up helps us achieve more favorable situations.

1012. Never giving up helps us achieve more records.

1013. Never giving up helps us achieve more efficient co operations.

1014. Never giving up helps us achieve more personal goals.

1015. Never giving up helps us achieve much good luck.

1016. Never giving up helps us achieve more favorable chances.

1017. Never giving up helps us achieve more performances.

Happy

1018. When we have realistic goals that we believe in and act with dedication to achieve them, some of us feel happy.

1019. Many of the people living from hand to mouth are not happy.

1020. When we achieve an objective we feel happy.

1021. The longer we are able to choose, prepare and carry out projects and objectives for the future, the more realistic the chances are of building a happy future.

1022. In most people's concerns regarding their objectives, their projects in different future aspects virtually do not exist neither in theoretical approaches nor do they speak about plans, projects, targets achieved. This fact makes their life one lived largely at random from hand to mouth, as many are not happy in the future ahead.

1023. Man can be happy in his life in a greater or smaller degree, depending on how he sees life, on how the philosophy of his life is, on the values he has.

1024. The fact that we do not have certain assets, accomplishments, etc. during certain periods of our life must not fret, consume, frustrate, make us unhappy, but it is necessary to enjoy what we have, what we have achieved, the projects that we have to achieve, the qualities, the skills that we have, etc.

1025. A man without a woman can not be truly happy or fulfilled.

1026. The true fulfillment of a woman is in a happy marriage with children.

1027. Having a happy marriage is a necessity for both men and women and especially for children.

1028. I am not saying that women should not be concerned with their outer beauty but to occupy themselves more with their inner beauty, to achieve and maintain a happy marriage. For these targets women fortunately have unlimited capacities but unfortunately very few use them.

1029. Women still have enormous reserves to prevent divorce and many unhappy marriages.

1030. A positive, effective way of life makes our life happy.

1031. To be happy in the future it is necessary to invest in the future to achieve our present and future objectives.

1032. Tact is a necessary quality to both spouses since it helps both to achieve and maintain a happy marriage.

1033. If I had a wife with many qualities, with many achievements, with more quality than me, with more and bigger achievements than me, I would enjoy it very much, I would be very happy, happy of her outstanding achievements, qualities, I would not feel complexed by her achievements, I would not feel disturbed, frustated, not envious, but I would want much more results and I would support her as I could to achieve her special objectives.

Happiness

1034. It is necessary and required of young people, for their good, happiness and future to establish and develop as many and as much powerful non-profit organizations, trade unions, political parties, institutions, legal entities, etc..as they can through which to promote their values, to contribute to their future, to promote and defend their present and future.

1035. It is necessary and obligatory for the young, for their happiness and their future, to act as one to be elected as many as they can in local, municipal, town, county councils, parliaments in countries, such as mayors of villages, towns and other institutions for which elections are made.

1036. Happiness has positive effects on health.

1037. Happiness is a must that all of us want, at all times.

1038. The effective man is effective in creating happiness.

1039. Happiness is a state desired by us all.

1040. If you know and apply the principles that lead us to happiness we are able to become happy.

1041. Often happiness does not come by itself.

1042. Our happiness depends a lot on the quality of our objectives.

1043. The continuous realistic establishing of our objectives helps us a lot in achieving our happiness.

1044. Happiness depends on each of us knowing how to choose, preparing and carring out the objectives for the future.

1045. The happiness of our future depends mostly on us.

1046. Unfortunately, neither people nor society address the future, are not concerned with the future that is so important to us, with how much it influences our future happiness.

1047. Women bring much in the life of a man, much joy, much happiness and satisfactions.

1048. It is always necessary to be fair, because fairness leads us to success and happiness.

1049. It is always necessary to be effective in any situation because in this way we are able to achieve more bigger or smaller successes and a lot of enjoyment, joy, happiness.

1050. Positive thinking makes us do positive deeds, makes us be able to solve our objectives, obtain smaller or greater successes, be appreciated, respected and esteemed, achieve and maintain our happiness, a happy marriage, etc.

1051. Those who have tact have more chances to achieve more joys, satisfactions and much more happiness.

1052. Establishing concrete, realistic, continuous objectives, immediate or futuristic is also the continuous and effective action to achieve and complete them continuously with other objectives. Needed for their fulfillment are factors that create a lot of happiness, without which we may never get to be happy.

1053. To achieve quality actions to become happy and maintain our happiness, it is necessary that every time we act to focus totally on that action, to be careful in everything we do. Any little distraction can have grater or smaller negative effects on our happiness. Because of this, our happiness totally depends on our overall happiness and on the quality of actions which we achieve, on the concentration and attention with which we perform them.

1054. A balanced life certainly leads us to happiness. It is worthwhile to make the necessary efforts to achieve a balanced life.

1055. The Internet has an enormous utility for the happiness of our family and of our children if we continuously use it to achieve happiness. For this reason it is good, necessary, useful and imperative that every family has one or more computers connected to the Internet based on the number of family members.

1056. At present, step by step, day by day we can get more information useful to us for the training and development of our wisdom. This makes us forever increase our chances of becoming happy rather than build, forge our own happiness. We have everything we need available to us in order to achieve happiness, it only depends on ourselves if we act effectively and persevering to achieve it.

1057. At the moment on the Internet and in the books written so far, we can find sufficient information to certainly help us build our own happiness in harmonious family relationships and with other people. It is necessary to establish the present and future that through their achievement make us happy and act effectively and with continuous dedication to attain them.

1058. Each man must act, support, and promote the formation and development of humanist economy for the sake and happiness of all people.

1059. Happiness cannot be replaced by anything. Happiness just happens.

1060. True happiness is only achieved together by a man and a woman.

1061. The inner beauty of a woman along with the inner beauty of a man contributes the most in achieving the joint happiness that each desires.

1062. The necessary efforts and the time needed to maintain a happy marriage is worth doing and respectively allocating because what a happy marriage can offer us we cannot obtain somewhere else and it is priceless for our good and happiness.

1063. The effects that happiness has on us are something only happiness can produce.

1064. The love of a woman given to a man is unique and has something special that makes it more apart and that creates happiness for the man, a happiness that only a woman can provide.

1065. Industriousness helps us and contributes a lot in achieving our happiness.

1066. Energetic men have more chances of achieving their happiness.

1067. The sense of responsibility contributes a lot in achieving our happiness.

1068. People with the sense of discipline have greater chances to achieve their own happiness.

1069. Most of those who wonder without a purpose in life have fewer chances to achieve their own happiness.

1070. An efficient man has also had a lot of happiness.

1071. Those who cherish their collaborators have a greater potential to achieve happiness.

1072. People with an innovative spirit have possibilities of achieving their happiness.

1073. The lack of neurotic symptoms helps us a lot to achieve our happiness.

1074. Very sociable people have greater chances to achieve their own happiness.

1075. People who are full of life and active have much more and greater chances to achieve their own happiness.

1076. Organizational sense has a great contribution in achieving our happiness.

1077. Those who build their life on rationally conscious bases have more chances to achieve happiness.

1078. Ignoring the truth is very harmful in the achievement of our happiness.

1079. Our happiness depends a lot on the formation, development, maintenance and usage of long term thinking.

Harmonious

1080. The harmonious development of our personality enormously helps us deal with all human troubles.

1081. Those who do not have hopes of creating hopes in the future need to harmoniously develop their personality.

1082. Humanist economy has the motivation to do good, to make a man happy, to offer him everything that he needs, to harmoniously develop his personality according to the surrounding environment.

1083. The economy of the harmonious development of human personality is an economy that is part of humanist economy.

1084. Humanist economy will contribute a lot in the harmonious development of human personality.

1085. Those who are independent have the possibility to harmoniously develop their personality.

1086. A man with self control harmoniously develops his personality.

1087. Correct relations with coworkers help us achieve more harmonious social relations.

1088. A realistic man in everything he does knows how to harmoniously develop his personality.

1089. A man who has practical values usually knows how to harmoniously develop his personality.

1090. A man who has a diversity of interests has much more and greater chances to harmoniously develop his personality.

1091. Working in teams of people with similar values is harmonious.

1092. Those who are preoccupied with creating an optimal cooperation in the team contribute a lot to creating a harmonious climate.

1093. Efficient positive human communication contributes a lot to achieving harmonious social relations.

1094. Those who do not have hopes, in order to create hopes for the future they need to connect with people who have harmoniously developed their personality.

1095. People who have had successes mostly know how to harmoniously develop their personality.

1096. Those without hopes for the future need to become friends with those who harmoniously develop their personality.

1097. When people sense each other they have more chances to achieve harmonious relations.

1098. When lovers sense each other they have more chances to achieve harmonious relations.

1099. When spouses sense each other they have more chances to achieve harmonious relations.

1100. When friends sense each other they have more chances to achieve harmonious relations.

Honest

1101. A great capacity of being honest with oneself must be rewarded.

1102. A great capacity of being honest with oneself helps us achieve more efficient co operations.

1103. A great capacity of being honest with oneself helps us maintain our happiness.

1104. A great capacity of being honest with oneself helps us become efficient.

1105. A great capacity of being honest with oneself helps us become more productive.

1106. A great capacity of being honest with oneself helps us achieve more performances.

1107. A great capacity of being honest with oneself helps us become enthusiastic.

1108. A great capacity of being honest with oneself helps us achieve more personal goals.

1109. A great capacity of being honest with oneself helps us become more efficient.

1110. A great capacity of being honest with oneself helps us become cautious.

1111. A great capacity of being honest with oneself helps us maintain our way of being liked.

1112. A great capacity of being honest with oneself helps us maintain our tolerance.

1113. A great capacity of being honest with oneself helps us become happier.

1114. A great capacity of being honest with oneself helps us maintain our way of being loving.

1115. A great capacity of being honest with oneself helps us maintain our humanity.

1116. A great capacity of being honest with oneself helps us become more practical.

1117. A great capacity of being honest with oneself helps us become humane.

1118. A great capacity of being honest with oneself helps us achieve more favorable chances.

1119. A great capacity of being honest with oneself helps us become more loving.

1120. A great capacity of being honest with oneself helps us become optimistic.

1121. A great capacity of being honest with oneself helps us become more pleasant.

1122. A great capacity of being honest with oneself helps us become practical.

1123. A great capacity of being honest with oneself helps us achieve more records.

1124. A great capacity of being honest with oneself helps us achieve more true friendships.

1125. A great capacity of being honest with oneself helps us maintain our way of being understanding.

Hope

1126. One hope can be a creator of another hope or of other hopes.

1127. Life without hope is a life left to chance.

1128. Hopes slow our aging.

1129. Hopes help us contribute to having more opportunities to meet more favorable circumstances.

1130. Sometimes hopes are verminous.

1131. Our future is very much influenced by our hopes.

1132. People who have hopes always have employment.

1133. Hopes make us keep our thinking in the long term.

1134. Hopes make us become more active.

1135. Hopes help us not be discouraged.

1136. Hopes help us create friends.

1137. Hopes are the creatives of joy.

1138. Co-development helps us create new hope.

1139. Hopes are creators of new roads.

1140. Successes create hope.

1141. The more and greater successes we obtain the more and greater hopes we form.

1142. The more experienced we are, the more hopes we form based on our experience.

1143. The more useful knowledge we have that can help us achieve our personal goals the more hopes we can form.

1144. Hopes make us more confident in the future.

1145. Hopes are the engines of progress.

1146. Hopes make us feel alive.

1147. Hopes give us energy.

1148. Hopes make us feel better.

1149. A life without hope is a sad one.

1150. A man without hopes is a pessimistic man.

1151. Life is much more beautiful when we have hopes.

1152. Hopes contribute to creating good humor.

1153. Our life has been given to us so that we live it, but not in any way, mocking it, at chance, but thoughtly, economisingly, planningly, with good sense, with hopes, with positive thoughts and actions, with humanities, with love, with dedication only with what does us and others good. Good luck. You will succeed if you respect what there is to be respected, what you very well know and what must be respected. Good luck again.

1154. Hopes prevent us to arrive in the state of despair.

1155. A man with practical values permanently has hopes most of the time.

1156. An optimistic man many times has many hopes.

1157. Hopes make people happy many times.

1158. Hopes often contribute to maintaining our state of health.

1159. When we have hope we feel happy.

1160. Those who do not have hope need to form and develop efficient thinking.

1161. Those who do not have hope, in order to form hopes in the future, they need to develop their positive enterprising spirit.

1162. Those who do not have hopes of creating hope in the future need to form their sense of fairness.

1163. Those who do not have hopes of creating hopes in the future need to harmoniously develop their personality.

Incredibly

1164. People on earth have sufficient resources to unite their huge forces, through solidarity, cooperation, co-development, perseverance, willpower, work, the Internet, the media, the mobile phone, etc., to install in record time in many places and situations normality instead of abnormalities. Start right now that you will always succeed for you are an invincible force, you can replace the abnormal with the normal in no matter what situations and places. Persevere until you succeed and if you need it, continually ask for help from other citizens of the planet that will join you to become incredibly many. Good luck. I am sure you will succeed.

1165. Human stupidity is incredibly dangerous most of the times.

1166. Humanist economy will take the place of present economies at an incredibly high rate.

1167. Humanist scientific knowledge, human living experience, stored in books, on the Internet, in the media, human qualities allow the achievement of an incredibly high number of happy marriages, but, unfortunately, many people do not give the time and the attention necessary to achieving and maintaining a happy marriage.

1168. There is incredibly much property in many states of the world. This is due to the inefficiency and the responsibility of state administration.

1169. There are enormously many people who do incredibly little to achieve a true mature love.

1170. There is an incredible number of people who do incredibly little to maintain their love.

1171. Negative attitudes can sometimes harm us incredibly much.

Ingenious

1172. Pessimism can be removed and replaced with optimism also through the contribution of the formation, development, maintenance and usage of ingenious behavior.

1173. Continuous self-motivation helps us become ingenious.

1174. Problems cannot be solved by the ideas that created them but also through the contribution of the formation, development, maintenance and usage of ingenious behavior.

1175. Our own happiness can be achieved and maintained also through the contribution of the formation, development, maintenance and usage of ingenious behavior.

1176. In order to prevent failures it is necessary to also form, develop, maintain and use ingenious behavior.

1177. Release from our self-imposed restrictions can be made also through the contribution of the formation, development, maintenance and usage of ingenious behavior.

1178. Stress can be prevented also through the formation, development, maintenance and usage of ingenious behavior.

1179. We can overcome the difficulties that we must overcome also through the help of the formation, development, maintenance and usage of ingenious behavior.

1180. Acting efficiently helps us become ingenious.

1181. Our happiness depends a lot also on the formation, development, maintenance and usage of ingenious behavior.

1182. The necessary qualities in achieving personal goals can be formed, developed, maintained and used also through the contribution of the formation, development, maintenance and usage of ingenious behavior.

1183. The radical transformation for the better of our life can be achieved also through the formation, development, maintenance and usage of ingenious behavior.

1184. The obstacles that prevent us from achieving our personal goals can be surpassed also through the contribution of the formation, development, maintenance and usage of ingenious behavior.

1185. Aspiring towards a more meaningful life can also be achieved through the formation, development, maintenance and usage of ingenious behavior.

1186. We can become stronger and we can not allow ourselves to be influenced by the world also through the contribution of the formation, development, maintenance and usage of ingenious behavior.

Intelectual

1187. We can form, develop and maintain the state of being ourselves also through the contribution of the formation, development, maintenance and usage of an intellectual behavior.

1188. The obstacles that prevent us from achieving our personal goals can be surpassed also through the contribution of the formation, development, maintenance and usage of intellectual behavior.

1189. We can overcome the difficulties that we must overcome also through the help of the formation, development, maintenance and usage of intellectual behavior.

1190. Stress can be prevented also through the formation, development, maintenance and usage of intellectual behavior.

1191. Our own happiness can be achieved and maintained also through the contribution of the formation, development, maintenance and usage of intellectual behavior.

1192. Positive experience can be achieved also through the contribution of the formation, development, maintenance and usage of intellectual behavior.

1193. In order to escape poverty it is necessary to also form, develop, maintain and use intellectual behavior.

1194. The radical transformation for the better of our life can be achieved also through the formation, development, maintenance and usage of intellectual behavior.

1195. Acting efficiently helps us become intellectual.

Joyful

1196. In order to rise up once again for the first time for the who knows what time it is necessary to also form, develop, maintain and use joyful behavior.

1197. Wisdom helps us become joyful.

1198. Our resistance to changing for the better can be overcome also through the contribution of the formation, development, maintenance and usage of joyful behavior.

1199. Rather than lamenting that we do not have successes it is more useful to also form, develop, maintain and use joyful behavior.

1200. Communication helps us become joyful.

1201. The necessary qualities in achieving personal goals can be formed, developed, maintained and used also through the contribution of the formation, development, maintenance and usage of joyful behavior.

1202. We can prevent some failures also through the contribution of the formation, development, maintenance and usage of joyful behavior.

1203. Responsibility helps us become joyful.

1204. Optimism helps us become joyful.

1205. The solutions to the problems we have or that we want to solve can be found also through the contribution of the formation, development, maintenance and usage of joyful behavior.

1206. Continuous self-motivation helps us become joyful.

1207. Obtaining more and greater successes can be achieved also through the contribution of the formation, development, maintenance, usage of a joyful behavior.

1208. Will helps us become joyful.

1209. Confidence in ourselves helps us become joyful.

1210. Release from our self-imposed restrictions can be made also through the contribution of the formation, development, maintenance and usage of joyful behavior.

1211. The obstacles that prevent us from achieving our personal goals can be surpassed also through the contribution of the formation, development, maintenance and usage of joyful behavior.

1212. Self-imposed discipline helps us become joyful.

1213. We can overcome the difficulties that we must overcome also through the help of the formation, development, maintenance and usage of joyful behavior.

1214. Aspiring towards a more meaningful life can also be achieved through the formation, development, maintenance and usage of joyful behavior.

1215. In achieving our successes a contribution is also brought by the formation, development, maintenance and usage of joyful behavior.

1216. Continuous self perfection helps us become joyful.

1217. We can prevent the falling apart of a happy marriage also through the contribution of the formation, development, maintenance and usage of joyful behavior.

1218. Our own happiness can be achieved and maintained also through the contribution of the formation, development, maintenance and usage of joyful behavior.

1219. The force of our ideas can be augmented also through the contribution of the formation, development, maintenance and usage of joyful behavior.

1220. Hopes can be created also through the contribution of the formation, development, maintenance and usage of joyful behavior.

Just

1221. A judge has many difficulties in achieving a justice quality act.

1222. In life it is necessary and required to develop positive feelings just because they only do us and others good.

1223. The judge who committed an injustice is necessary and required to answer criminaly, civily, financialy, for that injustice.

1224. If we do not have patience with us we can form it. It takes just a desire to act and to form it. Good luck.

1225. If we are right, any injustice we would do during the process must not, under any circumstances leave us defeated.

1226. If we are right, and have injustice in the law suits, it must give us greater powers to overcome injustice for us and to finally win justice.

1227. Justice can and must give us certainty to persevere until we win.

1228. People with skills do not envy the achievements of others but appreciate them to just their value.

1229. Sometimes unpleasant surprises appear just when you do not believe it.

1230. A happy marriage is something invaluable, unable to transliterate, which many of us know and we do not want to appreciate its just value, thus making a huge mistake and a very bad one.

1231. A judge who made a single injustice, has no moral right to judge. What to say to those who do daily tens of deeds of injustice, or annually thousands of deeds of injustice?

1232. It is necessary that the act of justice, the decisions and court rulings to be taken as much as possible with the help of computers.

1233. Today unfortunately the people of the planet just use a tiny part of the conquests and the achievements of science.

1234. We should never be careless about injustice.

1235. It is necessary and imperative that all countries take the necessary measures, continuously, day by day, to prevent any possible injustice.

1236. Any injustice should be removed in the shortest time.

1237. The one who has made an injustice is necessary to respond criminally and civilly for the injustice done.

1238. Some lawyers, many believe it, have participated actively and passively to the achievement of many injustices, illegalities of their clients, worldwide, in almost all the countries of the world.

1239. Often, if we had failures, we can learn much more from them than from successes, but this should not justify our failures, but look for the causes of failures and take preventive measures to stop our future failures.

Kind

1240. Kindness makes us more appreciated.

1241. Kindness must never lack.

1242. Kind people are unfortunately sometimes not considered.

1243. A woman with an inner beauty does much good to mankind.

1244. In order to follow and transform our personal goals into reality, it is necessary to also form, develop, maintain and use our kindness.

1245. In achieving our successes a contribution is also brought by the formation, development, maintenance and usage of kind behavior.

1246. Our resistance to changing for the better can be overcome also through the contribution of the formation, development, maintenance and usage of kind behavior.

1247. We can form, develop and maintain the state of being ourselves also through the contribution of the formation, development, maintenance and usage of a kind behavior.

1248. The force of our ideas can be augmented also through the contribution of the formation, development, maintenance and usage of kind behavior.

1249. The self efficient use of our time helps us become kind.

1250. Will helps us become kind.

1251. Optimism helps us become kind.

1252. The necessary qualities in achieving personal goals can be formed, developed,

maintained and used also through the contribution of the formation, development, maintenance and usage of kind behavior.

1253. In order to rise up once again for the first time for the who knows what time it is necessary to also form, develop, maintain and use kind behavior.

1254. Continuous self-control helps us become kind.

Knowledge

1255. We can face and overcome difficulties much easier in life with the more we accumulate from books, the Internet; more useful and necessary knowledge for surpassing the troubles we face in life.

1256. The positive knowledge is that which we accumulate form our way of life.

1257. As we accumulate more positive knowledge required to achieve our objectives the more we become more able to achieve then.

1258. We need, in order to accumulate knowledge very valuable to us and to achieving our objectives to listen to people who have achieved success, those who have knowledge that we need. No matter how we come in contact with them: directly, by radio, television, the Internet, it is very effective for us to take such useful, sometimes very useful information, knowledge to us for free.

1259. Through self-learning, we gain useful knowledge for avhieving personal projects.

1260. True friends help us greatly to accumulate more knowledge more quickly.

1261. Each of us with the help of the qualities that we have with that of those that we can shape and develop, of the various resources around the world, of the human experience and knowledge acquired in books, on the Internet, in publications, etc. we can be optimistic in our future in achieving a happy future. It is necessary to mobilize the will, qualities given to us with all our being to achieve the personal goal of making a happier future for us. Good luck to all. The ideas exposed by me can help very much, use them.

1262. In life, we have much more favorable circumstances if we have knowledge in many different areas. Because this is necessary for our own good to accumulate as long as we live as much knowledge in many areas as we can.

1263. Always in the creation and establishment of personal projects we must take into account our knowledge, qualities, abilities and our skills.

1264. If we establish personal projects for whose achievement we do not have the necessary knowledge, skills, qualities and abilities, we are very likely not to achieve them.

1265. We can form courage and grow it by more positive, effective and planned behaviors. Among these are the continued developments of our knowledge in as many areas that can influence directly or indirectly our personal goals as possible. Usually, we are afraid to face the unknown. The longer we accumulate more knowledge we need in areas in which we act, the more we become more courageous, more confident in ourselves, with more success. Therefore, it is necessary, useful and mandatory to develop what we need because it has multiple positive effects on us, besides the fact that we continuously increase our courage that we really need to achieve our personal goals.

1266. As we have more knowledge necessary to achieve our personal goals the more courage we have.

Listener

1267. The solutions to the problems we have or that we want to solve can be found also through the contribution of the formation, development, maintenance and usage of being a good listener behavior.

1268. The radical transformation for the better of our life can be achieved also through the formation, development, maintenance and usage of good listener behavior.

1269. The limits of achievement imposed by ourselves in our mind at a given moment can be overcome or eliminated also through the contribution of the formation, development, maintenance and usage of being a good listener behavior.

1270. Our resistance to changing for the better can be overcome also through the contribution of the formation, development, maintenance and usage of being a good listener behavior.

1271. Acting efficiently helps us become good listeners.

1272. Release from our self-imposed restrictions can be made also through the contribution of the formation, development, maintenance and usage of being a good listener behavior.

1273. Our happiness depends a lot also on the formation, development, maintenance and usage of good listener behavior.

1274. Will helps us become good listeners.

1275. Continuous self-control helps us become good listeners.

1276. We can form, develop and maintain the state of being ourselves also through the contribution of the formation, development, maintenance and usage of a behavior of being a good listener.

1277. The force of our ideas can be augmented also through the contribution of the formation, development, maintenance and usage of good listener behavior.

1278. Rather than lamenting that we do not have successes it is more useful to also form, develop, maintain and use a behavior of being a good listener.

1279. Continuous self perfection helps us become good listeners.

1280. Wisdom helps us become good listeners.

1281. We can become stronger and we can not allow ourselves to be influenced by the world also through the contribution of the formation, development, maintenance and usage of good listener behavior.

1282. Positive experience can be achieved also through the contribution of the formation, development, maintenance and usage of being a good listener behavior.

1283. In achieving our successes a contribution is also brought by the formation, development, maintenance and usage of good listener behavior.

Logical

1284. A psychological balance helps us greatly to continuously increase our efficiency.

1285. A psychological balance helps us prevent arguments.

1286. A psychological balance helps us make our life more beautiful.

1287. A psychological balance can be maintain once achieved through the proper nutrition of the person concerned, through education, intellectual work, perseverance, experience, willingness, physical exercises, etc.

1288. Those who believe that others are to blame for their mistakes are illogical in that rationality.

1289. It is risky to cooperate with people who sometimes have illogical rationalities.

1290. Luxury is an illogical waste of many and great resources.

1291. We can be stronger and we cannot let ourselves be influenced by the world also through the contribution of the formation, development, maintenance and usage of the ability to be logical.

1292. We can contribute to achieving our happiness also through the contribution of the formation, development, maintenance and usage of logical ideas.

1293. We can prevent some failures also through the contribution of the formation, development, maintenance and usage of the logical behaviors.

1294. Wrong ideas can be eliminated by using logical conceptions of life.

1295. We can avoid troubles through logical thinking.

1296. A correct thinking can be formed by using logical thinking.

1297. Doubts can be avoided through logical thinking.

1298. Pessimism can be removed through the contribution of the formation, development, maintenance and usage of logical thinking.

1299. The prevention of stress can be achieved also through the contribution of the formation, development, maintenance and usage of logical behavior.

1300. We can become stronger and we cannot let ourselves be influenced by the world also through the contribution of the formation, development, maintenance and usage of the ability to be logical.

1301. Doubts can be avoided through the formation, development, maintenance and usage of logical behaviors.

1302. Abilities can be formed with the contribution of logical behaviors.

1303. The restrictions we have imposed can be surpassed and eliminated also through the formation, development, maintenance and usage of the logical thinking.

1304. A great capacity of analyzing a situation logically helps us become cautious.

1305. A great capacity of analyzing a situation logically helps us achieve more records.

1306. A great capacity of analyzing a situation logically helps us maintain our productivity.

1307. Stress can be prevented also through the formation, development, maintenance and usage of logical behavior.

1308. A great capacity of analyzing a situation logically helps us achieve more efficient co operations.

1309. A great capacity of analyzing a situation logically must be supported.

1310. A great capacity of analyzing a situation logically must be rewarded.

1311. A great capacity of analyzing a situation logically helps us become more efficient.

1312. We can prevent some failures also through the contribution of the formation, development, maintenance and usage of logical behavior.

1313. A great capacity of analyzing a situation logically helps us maintain our way of being cautious.

1314. A great capacity of analyzing a situation logically helps us become happier.

1315. In order to rise up once again for the first time for the who knows what time it is necessary to also form, develop, maintain and use logical behavior.

1316. A great capacity of analyzing a situation logically helps us become loving.

1317. Pessimism can be removed and replaced with optimism also through the contribution of the formation, development, maintenance and usage of logical behavior.

Loving

1318. A great capacity of increasing creativity helps us maintain our way of being loving.

1319. A great capacity of investing efficiently helps us become loving.

1320. A great capacity of assuming the necessary risks for achieving personal goals helps us become more loving.

1321. A great capacity of analyzing a situation logically helps us become loving.

1322. A great capacity of more efficiently using financial means helps us become loving.

1323. A great capacity of teaching people helps us become more loving.

1324. A great capacity of using available resources helps us become more loving.

1325. A great capacity of managing life helps us become more loving.

1326. A great capacity of maintaining relationships with people helps us become more loving.

1327. A great capacity of using abilities helps us become more loving.

1328. A great capacity of investing efficiently helps us maintain our way of being loving.

1329. A great capacity of maintaining a positive efficient own lifestyle helps us become loving.

1330. A great capacity of anticipating helps us become loving.

1331. A great capacity of being understanding with people helps us become more loving.

185

1332. A great capacity of being honest with oneself helps us become loving.

1333. A great capacity of analyzing a situation logically helps us become more loving.

1334. A great capacity of making people more optimistic helps us become loving.

1335. A great capacity of appreciating people helps us become loving.

1336. A great capacity of not letting others lead one's life helps us become loving.

1337. A great capacity of maintaining relationships with people helps us maintain our way of being loving.

1338. A great capacity of thinking largely helps us become more loving.

1339. A great capacity of being brave helps us maintain our way of being loving.

1340. A great capacity of increasing creativity helps us become loving.

1341. A great capacity of using qualities helps us become more loving.

1342. Continuously making ourselves efficient helps us become loving.

1343. A great capacity of using attitudes helps us maintain our way of being loving.

1344. A great capacity of continuously enhancing performances helps us maintain our way of being loving.

1345. A great capacity of cherishing oneself helps us become more loving.

1346. A great capacity of cherishing oneself helps us maintain our way of being loving.

1347. A great capacity of assuming the necessary risks for achieving personal goals helps us maintain our way of being loving.

1348. A great capacity of being popular helps us become more loving.

1349. A great capacity of using available ideas helps us become more loving.

1350. A great capacity of being creative in order to solve great problems helps us become more loving.

1351. A great capacity of forming a positive own lifestyle helps us become loving.

1352. A great capacity of working hard helps us become loving.

1353. A great capacity of making people more optimistic helps us maintain our way of being loving.

1354. A great capacity of accomplishing strategies of applying thinking on a big scale helps us become loving.

1355. A great capacity of being as strong as possible helps us become loving.

1356. A great capacity of remaining involved in the same area with even greater objectives helps us become more loving.

1357. A great capacity of being flexible helps us maintain our way of being loving.

1358. A great capacity of having an even more energetic life helps us become loving.

1359. A great capacity of being tolerant with people helps us become more loving.

Loyal

1360. Rather than lamenting that we do not have successes it is more useful to also form, develop, maintain and use loyal behavior.

1361. Positive experience can be achieved also through the contribution of the formation, development, maintenance and usage of loyal behavior.

1362. Stress can be prevented also through the formation, development, maintenance and usage of loyal behavior.

1363. In order to prevent failures it is necessary to also form, develop, maintain and use loyal behavior.

1364. Our own happiness can be achieved and maintained also through the contribution of the formation, development, maintenance and usage of loyal behavior.

1365. Aspiring towards a more meaningful life can also be achieved through the formation, development, maintenance and usage of the loyal behavior.

1366. Hopes can be created also through the contribution of the formation, development, maintenance and usage of loyal behavior.

1367. Confidence in ourselves helps us become loyal.

1368. Pessimism can be removed and replaced with optimism also through the contribution of the formation, development, maintenance and usage of loyal behavior.

1369. Continuous self perfection helps us become loyal.

1370. Release from our self-imposed restrictions can be made also through the contribution of the formation, development, maintenance and usage of loyal behavior.

1371. In order to prevent not achieving our personal goals, it is necessary to also form, develop, maintain and use our loyal behavior.

1372. Optimism helps us become loyal.

1373. We can become stronger and we can not allow ourselves to be influenced by the world also through the contribution of the formation, development, maintenance and usage of the loyal behavior.

1374. Hope helps us become loyal.

1375. Continuous self-motivation helps us become loyal.

1376. Our happiness depends a lot also on the formation, development, maintenance and usage of the loyal behavior.

1377. In order to rise up once again for the first time for the who knows what time it is necessary to also form, develop, maintain and use loyal behavior.

1378. Our happiness depends a lot also on the formation, development, maintenance and usage of loyal behavior.

1379. Our future can be projected and achieved also through the contribution of the formation, development, maintenance and usage of the loyal behavior.

1380. Acting efficiently helps us become loyal.

1381. We can overcome the difficulties that we must overcome also through the help of the formation, development, maintenance and usage of the loyal behavior.

1382. The self efficient use of our time helps us become loyal.

1383. In achieving our successes a contribution is also brought by the formation, development, maintenance and usage of the loyal behavior.

1384. Communication helps us become loyal.

1385. Stress can be prevented also through the formation, development, maintenance and usage of the loyal behavior.

1386. We can prevent some failures also through the contribution of the formation, development, maintenance and usage of the loyal behavior.

1387. Some mistakes can be prevented also through the contribution of the formation, development, maintenance and usage of loyal behavior.

1388. The necessary qualities in achieving personal goals can be formed, developed, maintained and used also through the

contribution of the formation, development, maintenance and usage of loyal behavior.

1389. We can prevent some failures also through the contribution of the formation, development, maintenance and usage of loyal behavior.

1390. The force of our ideas can be augmented also through the contribution of the formation, development, maintenance and usage of loyal behavior.

1391. Creativity helps us become loyal.

1392. Our own happiness can be achieved and maintained also through the contribution of the formation, development, maintenance and usage of the loyal behavior.

1393. Problems cannot be solved by the ideas that created them but also through the contribution of the formation, development, maintenance and usage of the loyal behavior.

Mature

1394. Good humor can be maintained through a balanced life, a proper diet, education, intellectual exercises, psychical balance, perseverance, women, physical exercises, a value system in which we believe in and that we respect, positive activities, dynamism, social relations, friends, mature love, a happy marriage, etc.

1395. Good humor helps us maintain our mature love.

1396. Arguments between lovers stop the achievement of mature love.

1397. The more we know about the conditions and factors that contribute to achieving a mature love, the more chances we have to obtain that love.

1398. Mature love creates many satisfactions.

1399. Each of us needs to find all the qualities we have and develop them as much as possible in order to increase our chances of maintaining mature love.

1400. Humanist thinking helps us achieve a mature love.

1401. Mature love makes us desire life without death.

1402. Altruism helps us achieve a mature love.

1403. Fairness helps us a lot and increases our chances of achieving a mature love.

1404. A good fame helps us achieve mature love.

1405. Mature love prolongues our life.

1406. Mature love creates much happiness.

1407. Compliance with principles helps us achieve mature love.

Meticulous

1408. Continuous self-control helps us become meticulous.

1409. We can become stronger and we can not allow ourselves to be influenced by the world also through the contribution of the formation, development, maintenance and usage of meticulous behavior.

1410. In order to rise up once again for the first time for the who knows what time it is necessary to also form, develop, maintain and use meticulous behavior.

1411. Problems cannot be solved by the ideas that created them but also through the contribution of the formation, development, maintenance and usage of meticulous behavior.

1412. We can prevent some failures also through the contribution of the formation, development, maintenance and usage of meticulous behavior.

1413. Wisdom helps us become meticulous.

1414. The obstacles that prevent us from achieving our personal goals can be surpassed also through the contribution of the formation, development, maintenance and usage of meticulous behavior.

1415. Self-imposed discipline helps us become meticulous.

1416. Cherishing oneself helps us become meticulous.

1417. Stress can be prevented also through the formation, development, maintenance and usage of meticulous behavior.

1418. Communication helps us become meticulous.

1419. Creativity helps us become meticulous.

1420. Release from our self-imposed restrictions can be made also through the contribution of the formation, development, maintenance and usage of meticulous behavior.

1421. We can prevent the falling apart of a happy marriage also through the contribution of the formation, development, maintenance and usage of meticulous behavior.

1422. Continuous self perfection helps us become meticulous.

Morale

1423. An optimal morale increases our chances of not reaching panic situations.

1424. Good morale needs to be kept constant, every day, for as long as we live.

1425. Good morale helps us greatly to achieve a greater efficiency.

1426. Good morale helps us a lot to us achieve personal goals.

1427. Good morale helps us very much in achieving records.

1428. Good morale helps us very much to achieve effective co operations.

1429. As we have more experience, the more chances we have to achieve an optimal morale.

1430. If we do not have a good morale, we can shape it ourselves.

1431. Good morale greatly increases our chances of not getting in the situation of despair.

1432. Good morale greatly increases our ability to have self-control in any situation.

1433. Discipline enchains our morale.

Motivating

1434. We can prevent some failures also through the contribution of the formation, development, maintenance and usage of continuous self motivating behavior.

1435. In order to prevent not achieving our personal goals, it is necessary to also form, develop, maintain and use our continuous self motivating behavior.

1436. Release from our self-imposed restrictions can be made also through the contribution of the formation, development, maintenance and usage of continuous self-motivating behavior.

1437. We can prevent the falling apart of a happy marriage also through the contribution of the formation, development, maintenance and usage of continuous self-motivating behavior.

1438. We can contribute to the achievement of our greatest accomplishments also through the contribution of the formation, development, maintenance and usage of continuous self-motivating behavior.

1439. Some mistakes can be prevented also through the contribution of the formation, development, maintenance and usage of continuous self-motivating behavior.

1440. Aspiring towards a more meaningful life can also be achieved through the formation, development, maintenance and usage of continuous self motivating behavior.

1441. The limits of achievement imposed by ourselves in our mind at a given moment can be overcome or eliminated also through the contribution of the formation, development, maintenance and usage of continuous self-motivating behavior.

Objectivity

1442. Those who have the sense of objectivity become more efficient.

1443. Those who have the sense of objectivity make many exchanges of information.

1444. Those who have the sense of objectivity must be promoted.

1445. Those who have the sense of objectivity have the capacity to maintain efficient co-developments.

1446. Those who have the sense of objectivity are more credible.

1447. Those who have the sense of objectivity have more and greater chances to achieve a happy life.

1448. The sense of objectivity must be rewarded.

1449. Those who have the sense of objectivity more quickly achieve social relations.

1450. Those who have the sense of objectivity are also capable of maintaining a mature love.

1451. Those who have the sense of objectivity have more and greater chances to achieve happy marriages.

1452. The sense of objectivity increases the credibility of the person who has it.

1453. Those who have the sense of objectivity have more and greater chances to achieve a more beautiful life.

1454. The desire to make others happy can be accomplished through the contribution of the formation, development, maintenance and usage of the sense of social objectivity.

1455. Objectivity helps us more easily make friends.

1456. Objectivity helps us maintain true friendships.

Operative

1457. A cooperative man in activities more easily achieves efficient co-developments.

1458. A cooperative man in activities has a greater potential to achieve more and greater successes.

1459. A cooperative man in activities has much more chances to achieve true friendships.

1460. A cooperative man in activities achieves more efficient co operations.

1461. Our abilities can be formed, developed, maintained and used through the contribution of the formation, development, maintenance and usage of some cooperative behaviors.

1462. Obstacles that stop us from achieving our personal goals can be overcome also through the contribution of the formation, development, maintenance and usage of the ability to be cooperative in activities.

1463. In order to trace and transform our personal goals into reality it is necessary to form, develop, maintain and use the ability to be cooperative in the activities we have.

1464. Successful people are operative.

1465. Those who have high objectives in life are cooperative in activities.

1466. In order to pursue and transform our personal goals into reality we need to form, develop, maintain and use the ability to be cooperative in the activities that we have.

1467. Abilities can be formed, developed, maintained and used also through the contribution of the formation, development, maintenance and usage of cooperative behaviors.

1468. We can form, develop, maintain and use the state of being ourselves also through the ability of being cooperative.

1469. We can prevent stress also through the formation, development, maintenance and usage of cooperative behaviors.

1470. Our transformation for the better can be achieved through the ability to be cooperative.

1471. Cooperative people have greater chances to achieve happy marriages.

1472. Cooperative people are selfless.

1473. Cooperative people have greater chances to achieve more efficient co operations.

1474. Cooperative people are more likely to achieve more personal goals.

1475. Cooperative people are less selfish.

1476. Efficient friendships can help us become more cooperative.

Passionately

1477. Those who live their life passionately have greater chances to achieve efficient co operations.

1478. Those who passionately live their life have greater chances to find the right partner for life.

1479. Those who live life passionately and not at random have a great ability to succeed in life.

1480. Those who live life passionately and not at random have much more chances to achieve their desired efficient co operations.

1481. Those who live life passionately and not at random usually have a greater ability to find the right partner for life.

1482. People who do not have hopes, in order to create hopes need to connect with people who have succeeded in escaping the state of apathy and the lack of desire to live for the state of losing their life passionately.

1483. Those who live life passionately and not at random have a greater ability to contribute more to achieving the greater good.

1484. Those who live life passionately and not at random have a greater capacity to achieve more and greater outstanding performances.

1485. Those who live life passionately and not at random have a greater ability to achieve more and greater successes.

1486. Those who live life passionately and not at random have a greater ability to achieve their personal goals.

1487. Those who live life passionately and not at random have a special ability to maintain mature love.

1488. Those who live life passionately and not at random have a greater capacity to maintain a happy marriage.

1489. Those who live their life passionately and not at random have more chances to achieve true friendships.

1490. Those who live their life passionately and not at random have a greater ability to maintain their desire efficient co-developments.

1491. Those who live their life passionately have a greater ability to develop.

1492. Those who live their life passionately have a greater capacity to achieve the social relations they desire.

1493. Those who live their life passionately have a greater ability to achieve a happy life.

1494. Those who live life passionately and not at random must be rewarded.

1495. Those who passionately live their life have more chances to maintain their desired social relations.

1496. Those who live life passionately have a greater ability to achieve a more beautiful life.

1497. Those who live their life passionately must be promoted.

1498. Those who live their life passionately have the ability to prevent many failures.

1499. Those who live life passionately and not at random make fewer mistakes.

1500. Those who live life passionately and not at random have a great ability to achieve their own happiness.

1501. Those who live life passionately and not at random have the ability to maintain the efficient co operations they desire.

Patient

1502. Confidence in ourselves helps us become patient.

1503. Some mistakes can be prevented also through the contribution of the formation, development, maintenance and usage of patient behavior.

1504. Hope helps us become patient.

1505. Positive experience can be achieved also through the contribution of the formation, development, maintenance and usage of patient behavior.

1506. Continuous self-motivation helps us become patient.

1507. Wisdom helps us become patient.

1508. The obstacles that prevent us from achieving our personal goals can be surpassed also through the contribution of the formation, development, maintenance and usage of patient behavior.

1509. We can prevent some failures also through the contribution of the formation, development, maintenance and usage of patient behavior.

1510. In order to escape poverty it is necessary to also form, develop, maintain and use patient behavior.

1511. In order to rise up once again for the first time for the who knows what time it is necessary to also form, develop, maintain and use patient behavior.

1512. We can prevent the falling apart of a happy marriage also through the contribution of the formation, development, maintenance and usage of patient behavior.

1513. In order to prevent failures it is necessary to also form, develop, maintain and use patient behavior.

1514. Release from our self-imposed restrictions can be made also through the contribution of the formation, development, maintenance and usage of patient behavior.

1515. In order to prevent not achieving our personal goals, it is necessary to also form, develop, maintain and use our patient behavior.

1516. We can form, develop and maintain the state of being ourselves also through the contribution of the formation, development, maintenance and usage of a patient behavior.

1517. Self-imposed discipline helps us become patient.

1518. We can contribute to the achievement of our greatest accomplishments also through the contribution of the formation, development, maintenance and usage of patient behavior.

1519. We can become stronger and we can not allow ourselves to be influenced by the world also through the contribution of the formation, development, maintenance and usage of patient behavior.

1520. The self efficient use of our time helps us become patient.

1521. Communication helps us become patient.

Peaceful

1522. Confidence in ourselves helps us become peaceful.

1523. The force of our ideas can be augmented also through the contribution of the formation, development, maintenance and usage of peaceful behavior.

1524. We can form, develop and maintain the state of being ourselves also through the contribution of the formation, development, maintenance and usage of a peaceful behavior.

1525. We can become stronger and we can not allow ourselves to be influenced by the world also through the contribution of the formation, development, maintenance and usage of peaceful behavior.

1526. Creativity helps us become peaceful.

1527. Stress can be prevented also through the formation, development, maintenance and usage of peaceful behavior.

1528. Our resistance to changing for the better can be overcome also through the contribution of the formation, development, maintenance and usage of peaceful behavior.

1529. Hope helps us become peaceful.

1530. The limits of achievement imposed by ourselves in our mind at a given moment can be overcome or eliminated also through the contribution of the formation, development, maintenance and usage of peaceful behavior.

1531. In order to prevent not achieving our personal goals, it is necessary to also form, develop, maintain and use our peaceful behavior.

1532. Aspiring towards a more meaningful life can also be achieved through the formation, development, maintenance and usage of peaceful behavior.

1533. We can prevent some failures also through the contribution of the formation, development, maintenance and usage of peaceful behavior.

1534. Acting efficiently helps us become peaceful.

1535. Communication helps us become peaceful.

1536. In order to escape poverty it is necessary to also form, develop, maintain and use peaceful behavior.

1537. Cherishing oneself helps us become peaceful.

1538. Continuous self-motivation helps us become peaceful.

Perseverant

1539. Positive experience can be achieved also through the contribution of the formation, development, maintenance and usage of perseverant behavior.

1540. Some mistakes can be prevented also through the contribution of the formation, development, maintenance and usage of perseverant behavior.

1541. Release from our self-imposed restrictions can be made also through the contribution of the formation, development, maintenance and usage of perseverant behavior.

1542. We can prevent the falling apart of a happy marriage also through the contribution of the formation, development, maintenance and usage of perseverant behavior.

1543. The limits of achievement imposed by ourselves in our mind at a given moment can be overcome or eliminated also through the contribution of the formation, development, maintenance and usage of perseverant behavior.

1544. The obstacles that prevent us from achieving our personal goals can be surpassed also through the contribution of the formation, development, maintenance and usage of perseverant behavior.

Planning

1545. In order to pursue and transform our personal goals into reality we need to form, develop, maintain and use the sense of efficiently planning our actions.

1546. We can contribute to achieving our happiness also through the contribution of the formation, development, maintenance and usage of the conception of efficiently planning our positive actions.

1547. In order to pursue and transform our personal goals into reality we need to form, develop, maintain and use the sense of efficient planning.

1548. Emancipation from self imposed restrictions can be made through the formation, development and maintenance of planning our actions.

1549. The state of psychical discomfort can be removed also through the formation, development and maintenance of the sense of planning positive actions.

1550. In order to prevent failures it is necessary that we form, develop, maintain and use the sense of the efficient planning of actions.

1551. In achieving successes a contribution is brought by the formation, development, maintenance and usage of the sense of efficiently planning actions.

1552. Forming wrong ideas can be prevented also through the formation, development, maintenance and usage of the sense of efficiently planning positive actions.

1553. In order to pursue and transform positive objectives into reality it is necessary to form, develop, maintain and use the sense of efficient planning.

1554. Discipline can be formed, developed and maintained by efficiently planning actions.

1555. In order to succeed it is necessary to form, develop, maintain and use the sense of efficiently planning our actions.

1556. Creative ability can be achieved also through the contribution of the formation, development, maintenance and usage of the sense of efficient planning.

1557. Successes in life can also be achieved thanks to efficiently planning our actions.

Practical

1558. A great capacity of making people more optimistic helps us become more practical.

1559. A great capacity of making people more optimistic helps us become practical.

1560. A great capacity of adopting visions helps us become practical.

1561. A great capacity of being understanding with people helps us become more practical.

1562. Hope helps us become practical.

1563. A great capacity of forming a positive own lifestyle helps us maintain our way of being practical.

1564. A great capacity of forming a positive own lifestyle helps us become more practical.

1565. A great capacity of investing efficiently helps us become more practical.

1566. A great capacity of being wise helps us become practical.

Preventive

1567. Preventive actions are very effective in most cases.

1568. Preventive thinking is extremely necessary.

1569. Preventive and long term thinking are increasingly necessary for each of us for "n" reasons.

1570. Thinking is a preventive factor that helps us prevent a lot of mistakes.

1571. Those who have a preventive thinking have more chances to realize their personal goals than those who do not have a preventive thinking.

1572. To succeed in life, we need preventive thinking.

1573. To achieve and maintain a happy marriage we need to have and use a preventive thinking.

1574. Large and small failures could be avoided if preventive thinking is used.

1575. Many divorces could have been avoided if both spouses had had a preventive thinking.

1576. All happy marriages owe their happiness to the fact that spouses have a preventive thinking.

1577. Effective preventive actions are very efficient in most cases.

1578. Effective preventive thinking can create many ideas that become effective preventive measures and can contribute greatly to the achievement of personal goals.

1579. In order not to hinder the achievement of our happiness it is necessary not to consume ourselves for any trouble, accident, etc.. no matter how big it would be, it does not help us solve anything but instead consumes our resources in an inefficient, unnecessary way. Logically, it is necessary to see that catastrophe, mistake, that failure and to:

Take the necessary measures to stop the negative effects of that unhappiness, mistake, failure. both for us and for others.

Seek and detect whether it is possible not to repeat the catastrophe so to take the necessary preventive measures, not to repeat it.

Take all possible necessary measures to prevent the causes that led to the catastrophe, etc. or which may lead to other kinds of misfortune.

1580. Preventive actions help us prevent very much possible mistakes.

1581. Continuously, every day it is necessary to realize preventive actions that we need, for as long as we live.

1582. Establishing preventive measures is required continuously, day by day, but we need to be an objective person.

1583. Preventive actions help us very much to prevent many negative effects of our actions.

1584. Preventive actions help us to prevent a lot more inefficient actions.

1585. Preventive actions help us to prevent much more possible failures.

1586. Preventive actions help us greatly to prevent many possible accidents.

1587. Preventive actions help us very much to prevent many unpleasant surprises.

1588. Preventive actions help us very much to keep our marriage happy.

1589. Preventive actions help us very much to keep mature love.

1590. Often, if we had failures, we can learn much more from them than from successes, but this should not justify our failures, but look for the causes of failures and take preventive measures to stop our future failures.

1591. Each of us needs to pay the attention and time needed to develop preventive thinking.

1592. Preventive actions help prevent many blunder.

1593. Preventive thinking is necessary to be developed continuously for as long as we live as to prevent everything that might harm us.

1594. Each parent is required to form and develop their children's preventive thinking.

1595. Preventive actions help prevent many mistakes.

1596. Often, if we have a failure we can learn more from it than from a success, but this does not have to justify failure, we must look for the causes of that failure and take preventive measures to stop other failures.

1597. Preventive actions help us and contribute to achieving a happy marriage.

1598. Preventive thinking needs to be formed, developed and used continuously for as long as we live.

1599. Preventive thinking helps us and contributes to having more and greater successes.

1600. Preventive thinking helps us develop harmonious efficient co-developments.

1601. Preventive actions help us achieve our personal goals.

1602. Preventive actions help prevent many inefficient actions.

1603. Without using our preventive thinking we cannot achieve our desired future.

1604. Using our preventive thinking is a necessity.

1605. Using our preventive thinking is an engine of development of progress in many fields of activity.

1606. Using preventive thinking increases our chances to succeed.

1607. Using preventive thinking increases our participation in achieving the greater good.

1608. Using preventive thinking helps us a lot in life.

1609. Preventive thinking must be promoted.

1610. Using preventive thinking helps us achieve our own happiness.

1611. Using preventive thinking contributes to the development of global thinking.

1612. Using preventive thinking helps in the achievement of some positive social relations.

1613. Preventive thinking contributes a lot in achieving efficient co operations.

1614. Using preventive thinking requires many exchanges of information.

1615. Preventive thinking must be maintained.

1616. People who have had successes mostly have a preventive thinking.

1617. Positive thinking helps us a lot to continuously be preventive.

1618. Preventive thinking is a necessity.

1619. Preventive thinking has a great contribution in achieving the desired future.

1620. Using preventive thinking is an obligation.

1621. The use of preventive thinking is an engine of development in all areas of activity.

1622. Using preventive thinking makes us more credible.

1623. Using preventive thinking makes us commit fewer mistakes.

1624. Preventive thinking must be rewarded.

1625. Humanist economy will greatly develop preventive economy.

1626. A man who knows how to protect himself permanently takes preventive measures.

1627. Forming wrong ideas about what is happening to us can be prevented also through the contribution of the formation, development, maintenance and usage of preventive thinking.

1628. We can overcome the difficulties that we need to overcome also through the formation, development and maintenance of preventive thinking.

1629. Those who are remarkably gifted many times have a preventive thinking.

1630. People with human social behaviors need to have a preventive thinking as well.

1631. Those who have high objectives in life mostly have a preventive thinking.

1632. People who know how to take quality decisions also have a preventive thinking.

1633. Those who do not have hopes, in order to create hopes for the future they need to connect with people with preventive thinking.

1634. The sense of achieving quality in everything we do develops our preventive thinking.

1635. People with no hopes for the future must form and develop their preventive thinking.

1636. The desire to make others happy can be really achieved also through the contribution of the formation, development, maintenance and usage of preventive ideas.

1637. Forming wrong ideas can be prevented also through the formation, development, maintenance and usage of preventive thinking.

1638. In order to pursue and transform our objectives into reality it is necessary to form, develop, maintain and use preventive thinking as well.

1639. Emancipation from self imposed restrictions can be made through the formation, development and maintenance of preventive thinking.

1640. Preventing the formation of doubts can also be achieved through the formation, development, maintenance and usage of a preventive life conception.

1641. Finding the meaning of our lives can be achieved also through the contribution of the formation, development, maintenance and usage of a preventive life conception.

1642. Those who do not think enough need to form, develop, maintain and use there preventive thinking.

1643. We can overcome difficulties that we must overcome also through the formation, development and maintenance of preventive thinking.

1644. In order to pursue and transform our personal goals into reality we need to form and develop preventive thinking as well.

1645. We can prevent some failures also through the formation of the formation, development, maintenance and usage of preventive behaviors.

1646. Doubts can be removed using preventive thinking.

1647. The desire to make others happy can be accomplished through the contribution of the formation, development, maintenance and usage of preventive ideas.

1648. Forming wrong ideas can be prevented through the contribution of the formation, development, maintenance and usage of preventive thinking.

1649. In order to pursue and transform positive objectives into reality it is necessary to form, develop, maintain and use preventive thinking.

1650. In order to change into reality it is necessary to form, develop, maintain and use preventive thinking.

1651. We can broaden our horizon by using preventive life conceptions.

1652. Aspiring towards a more meaningful life can be achieved also through the contribution of the formation, development, maintenance and usage of a preventive conception.

1653. Preventing the formation of doubts can be achieved also through the formation, development, maintenance and usage of preventive thinking.

1654. Successes in life can also be achieved thanks to preventive thinking.

1655. A great capacity of continuously overcoming boundaries helps us become more preventive.

1656. A great capacity of learning in order to achieve successes helps us become more preventive.

1657. A great capacity of working hard helps us become more preventive.

1658. Confidence in ourselves helps us become preventive.

1659. A great capacity of making people more optimistic helps us become more preventive.

1660. A great capacity of being flexible helps us become more preventive.

1661. The desire to be grand helps us become more preventive.

1662. A great capacity of succeeding in every way helps us become more preventive.

1663. A great capacity of rapid instruction helps us become more preventive.

1664. A great capacity of positively influencing people helps us become more preventive.

1665. A great capacity of being as strong as possible helps us become more preventive.

1666. A great capacity of applying strategies of thinking big style helps us become more preventive.

1667. A great capacity of maintaining a positive efficient own lifestyle helps us become more preventive.

1668. Continuous self-motivation helps us become preventive.

1669. A great capacity of using a value system helps us become more preventive.

1670. A great capacity of gathering our energies helps us become more preventive.

1671. A great capacity of using available resources helps us become more preventive.

1672. A great capacity of appreciating people helps us become more preventive.

1673. A great capacity of using each failure to achieve successes helps us become more preventive.

1674. A great capacity of increasing creativity helps us become more preventive.

1675. A great capacity of establishing even greater personal goals helps us become more preventive.

1676. A great capacity of having one's own principles and not letting one be influenced by the negative opinions of others helps us become more preventive.

1677. A great capacity of teaching people helps us become more preventive.

1678. A great capacity of making great plans helps us become more preventive.

1679. A great capacity of being popular helps us become more preventive.

1680. A great capacity of using available knowledge helps us become more preventive.

1681. A great capacity of maintaining relationships with people helps us become more preventive.

1682. A great capacity of assuming the necessary risks for success helps us become more preventive.

1683. A great capacity of encouraging people helps us become more preventive.

1684. A great capacity of investing efficiently helps us become more preventive.

1685. A great capacity of being convincing helps us become more preventive.

1686. A great capacity of achieving what was proposed helps us become more preventive.

1687. A great capacity of being wise helps us become more preventive.

1688. A great capacity of more efficiently using time helps us become more preventive.

1689. A great capacity of establishing high personal goals helps us become more preventive.

1690. A great capacity of increasing self confidence helps us become more preventive.

1691. Continuous self perfection helps us become preventive.

1692. A great capacity of being creative in order to solve great problems helps us become more preventive.

1693. A great capacity of continuously enhancing performances helps us become more preventive.

1694. A great capacity of being tolerant with people helps us become more preventive.

1695. A great capacity of assuming the necessary risks for achieving great successes helps us become more preventive.

1696. A great capacity of fighting back helps us become more preventive.

1697. A great capacity of establishing great personal goals helps us become more preventive.

1698. A great capacity of maintaining self confidence helps us become more preventive.

1699. A great capacity of anticipating helps us become more preventive.

1700. A great capacity of using qualities helps us become more preventive.

1701. A great capacity of facing one's own life helps us become more preventive.

1702. A great capacity of persevering until finding creative solutions helps us become more preventive.

1703. A great capacity of drawing attention helps us become more preventive.

1704. A great capacity of more efficiently using financial means helps us become more preventive.

1705. A great capacity of self-surpassing helps us become more preventive.

1706. A great capacity of analyzing a situation logically helps us become more preventive.

1707. A great capacity of continuous self perfection helps us become more preventive.

1708. The dream to the grand helps us become more preventive.

1709. A great capacity of using attitudes helps us become more preventive.

1710. A great capacity of assuming the necessary risks for achieving personal goals helps us become more preventive.

1711. Adaptation helps us become more preventive.

1712. A great capacity of using each personal mistake to achieve successes helps us become more preventive.

1713. A great capacity of achieving human relationships helps us become more preventive.

1714. A great capacity of accomplishing strategies of applying thinking on a big scale helps us become more preventive.

1715. A great capacity of being honest with oneself helps us become more preventive.

1716. A great capacity of remaining involved in the same area with even greater objectives helps us become more preventive.

1717. A great capacity of continuously positively transforming life helps us become more preventive.

1718. A great capacity of doing what is best helps us become more preventive.

1719. A great capacity of preventing situations of being deceived helps us become more preventive.

1720. A great capacity of forming a positive own lifestyle helps us become more preventive.

1721. Hope helps us become preventive.

1722. A great capacity of not letting others lead one's life helps us become more preventive.

1723. A great capacity of creating one's own safety helps us become more preventive.

1724. A great capacity of understanding others helps us become more preventive.

1725. A great capacity of using abilities helps us become more preventive.

1726. A great capacity of adopting visions helps us become more preventive.

1727. A great capacity of using available ideas helps us become more preventive.

1728. A great capacity of cherishing oneself helps us become more preventive.

1729. A great capacity of learning how to achieve personal goals helps us become more preventive.

1730. A great capacity of being brave helps us become more preventive.

1731. A great capacity of enjoying work helps us become more preventive.

1732. A great capacity of being oneself helps us become more preventive.

1733. A great capacity of having an even more energetic life helps us become more preventive.

1734. Perseverance helps us become preventive.

1735. A great capacity of being understanding with people helps us become more preventive.

1736. A great capacity of being friendly helps us become more preventive.

1737. A great capacity of thinking largely helps us become more preventive.

1738. A great capacity of managing life helps us become more preventive.

1739. A great capacity of using each injustice received in order to achieve successes helps us become more preventive.

1740. A great capacity of dealing with pressures, no matter how great they are, helps us become more preventive.

Productivity

1741. Mental self-development enormously increases our efficiency and productivity of our thinking for as long as we live, on a continuous basis.

1742. Mental self-development enormously increases with much efficiency, productivity our actions with tremendous positive effects so that we can cooperate with others and with society.

1743. Discipline increases productivity.

1744. Efficient inter human relations increase our productivity.

1745. A great capacity of teaching people helps us maintain our productivity.

1746. A great capacity of fighting back helps us maintain our productivity.

1747. A great capacity of analyzing a situation logically helps us maintain our productivity.

1748. A great capacity of using each failure to achieve successes helps us maintain our productivity.

1749. A great capacity of enjoying work helps us maintain our productivity.

1750. A great capacity of learning in order to achieve successes helps us maintain our productivity.

1751. A great capacity of more efficiently using financial means helps us maintain our productivity.

1752. A great capacity of using qualities helps us maintain our productivity.

1753. A great capacity of establishing high personal goals helps us maintain our productivity.

1754. A great capacity of continuous self perfection helps us maintain our productivity.

1755. A great capacity of working hard helps us maintain our productivity.

1756. A great capacity of using attitudes helps us maintain our productivity.

1757. A great capacity of drawing attention helps us maintain our productivity.

1758. The desire to be grand helps us maintain our productivity.

1759. A great capacity of being creative in order to solve great problems helps us maintain our productivity.

1760. A great capacity of being understanding with people helps us maintain our productivity.

1761. A great capacity of facing one's own life helps us maintain our productivity.

1762. A great capacity of continuously overcoming boundaries helps us maintain our productivity.

1763. A great capacity of thinking largely helps us maintain our productivity.

1764. A great capacity of making great plans helps us maintain our productivity.

1765. A great capacity of establishing even greater personal goals helps us maintain our productivity.

1766. A great capacity of doing what is best helps us maintain our productivity.

1767. A great capacity of assuming the necessary risks for achieving great successes helps us maintain our productivity.

1768. A great capacity of being convincing helps us maintain our productivity.

1769. A great capacity of making people more optimistic helps us maintain our productivity.

1770. A great capacity of continuously enhancing performances helps us maintain our productivity.

1771. A great capacity of cherishing oneself helps us maintain our productivity.

1772. A great capacity of using each injustice received in order to achieve successes helps us maintain our productivity.

1773. A great capacity of using a value system helps us maintain our productivity.

1774. A great capacity of being flexible helps us maintain our productivity.

1775. A great capacity of having one's own principles and not letting one be influenced by the negative opinions of others helps us maintain our productivity.

1776. A great capacity of being wise helps us maintain our productivity.

1777. Adaptation helps us maintain productivity.

1778. A great capacity of remaining involved in the same area with even greater objectives helps us maintain our productivity.

1779. A great capacity of encouraging people helps us maintain our productivity.

1780. A great capacity of adopting visions helps us maintain our productivity.

1781. A great capacity of persevering until finding creative solutions helps us maintain our productivity.

1782. A great capacity of anticipating helps us maintain our productivity.

1783. A great capacity of establishing great personal goals helps us maintain our productivity.

1784. A great capacity of being oneself helps us maintain our productivity.

1785. A great capacity of understanding others helps us maintain our productivity.

1786. A great capacity of increasing self confidence helps us maintain our productivity.

1787. The dream to the grand helps us maintain our productivity.

1788. A great capacity of succeeding in every way helps us maintain our productivity.

1789. A great capacity of maintaining self confidence helps us maintain our productivity.

1790. A great capacity of gathering our energies helps us maintain our productivity.

1791. A great capacity of applying strategies of thinking big style helps us maintain our productivity.

1792. A great capacity of achieving human relationships helps us maintain our productivity.

1793. A great capacity of achieving what was proposed helps us maintain our productivity.

1794. A great capacity of preventing situations of being deceived helps us maintain our productivity.

1795. A great capacity of having an even more energetic life helps us maintain our productivity.

1796. A great capacity of using each personal mistake to achieve successes helps us maintain our productivity.

1797. A great capacity of being popular helps us maintain our productivity.

1798. A great capacity of learning how to achieve personal goals helps us maintain our productivity.

1799. A great capacity of maintaining relationships with people helps us maintain our productivity.

1800. A great capacity of investing efficiently helps us maintain our productivity.

1801. A great capacity of not letting others lead one's life helps us maintain our productivity.

1802. A great capacity of being as strong as possible helps us maintain our productivity.

1803. A great capacity of managing life helps us maintain our productivity.

1804. A great capacity of assuming the necessary risks for achieving personal goals helps us maintain our productivity.

1805. A great capacity of rapid instruction helps us maintain our productivity.

1806. A great capacity of continuously positively transforming life helps us maintain our productivity.

1807. A great capacity of using available knowledge helps us maintain our productivity.

1808. A great capacity of forming a positive own lifestyle helps us maintain our productivity.

1809. A great capacity of self-surpassing helps us maintain our productivity.

1810. A great capacity of being tolerant with people helps us maintain our productivity.

1811. A great capacity of appreciating people helps us maintain our productivity.

1812. A great capacity of using abilities helps us maintain our productivity.

1813. A great capacity of assuming the necessary risks for success helps us maintain our productivity.

1814. A great capacity of maintaining a positive efficient own lifestyle helps us maintain our productivity.

1815. A great capacity of accomplishing strategies of applying thinking on a big scale helps us maintain our productivity.

1816. A great capacity of increasing creativity helps us maintain our productivity.

1817. A great capacity of using available resources helps us maintain our productivity.

1818. A great capacity of using available ideas helps us maintain our productivity.

1819. A great capacity of more efficiently using time helps us maintain our productivity.

1820. A great capacity of dealing with pressures, no matter how great they are, helps us maintain our productivity.

1821. A great capacity of positively influencing people helps us maintain our productivity.

1822. A great capacity of being honest with oneself helps us maintain our productivity.

1823. A great capacity of creating one's own safety helps us maintain our productivity.

1824. A great capacity of being friendly helps us maintain our productivity.

1825. A great capacity of being brave helps us maintain our productivity.

Qualities

1826. Each of us surely has a higher or lower number of qualities. It is for our own good and for our happiness to discover them and then to use them as much as we can in order to make us happy.

1827. Each of us surely has a higher or lower number of qualities. It is for our own good and for our happiness to discover them and then to use them as much as we can in order to make us happy.

1828. Each of us has a bigger or smaller number of qualities.

1829. It is never too late to self-develop certain qualities.

1830. It is necessary at all times to develop our human qualities.

1831. Those that have more qualities have more opportunities to make themselves happy.

1832. Our qualities make a lot of us very happy.

1833. Human qualities contribute the most to human success.

1834. Young people of the world's states, unfortunately, do not use their capacities and qualities, skills, abilities, attitudes, knowledge, and the enormous energy that they have, their enthusiasm and optimism, which are positive things, the desire of affirmation and of making achievements in order to participate in the activity of communal, municipal, departmental, regional councils of counties, of parliaments, of governments, etc..

1835. Human qualities contribute the most to human successes.

1836. Human qualities make a lot of people happy.

1837. Persons with many qualities are respected.

1838. Persons with many qualities are valued.

1839. Persons with many qualities are more likely to achieve more successes than those who have fewer skills.

1840. Persons with many qualities have very big chances to achieve successes.

1841. A man with qualities is appreciated.

1842. The more qualities we have, the more and greater opportunities we have to achieve more successes.

1843. The fact that we do not have certain assets, accomplishments, etc. during certain periods of our life must not fret, consume, frustrate, make us unhappy, but it is necessary to enjoy what we have, what we have achieved, the projects that we have to achieve, the qualities, the skills that we have, etc.

1844. I esteem women very much, appreciate and respect them very much for what they are, for the special qualities that they have.

1845. Men need to appreciate, respect all the qualities of women no matter what the situation is, even in this situation when these have more qualities than them.

1846. Many of us have the qualities and skills necessary to grow and be educated properly, but unfortunately not all have the time needed and they make big, very big mistakes, which later are not good for anything that we did. Warning also to successful people who can prevent this mistake.

1847. Each of us needs to discover all his qualities and to grow as much as possible in order to increase our chances of achieving more and greater successes.

1848. Individual qualities help and contribute greatly to achieving successes.

1849. We must be happy with the qualities that we have and develop them continuously, day by day, and use them effectively so that we are effective.

1850. Each of us is necessary to discover the qualities and to grow them as much as possible in order to increase our chances of achieving our personal goals.

1851. The more qualities needed to achieve personal goals we have the more chances and opportunities we have to make fewer mistakes.

1852. Intellectual qualities are also an effect of education.

1853. Intellectual qualities can be developed continuously, day by day, for as long as we live.

1854. Intellectual qualities are more important to succeed in life.

1855. Intellectual qualities help us the most to achieve many personal goals.

1856. Intellectual qualities help us achieve effective co operations.

1857. Courage is also created by qualities that you have as a person.

1858. Moral qualities help us keep our happy marriage.

1859. Self-knowledge helps us form the qualities that we do not have but that we need.

1860. Children are suffering very high mental trauma when parents divorce. Dear parents, if you have children, before the divorce, look to find solutions to prevent the divorce and to achieve a happy marriage for both you and your children. To be sure you have the qualities required and can perform a real, happy marriage, if both of you cooperate sincerely, if you are both more tolerant with each other, if you make all the compromises necessary, if you do not worry about all kinds of complexes, if you want to understand the other, if you lose pride to nonsense, if you do what is necessary for both spouses and children to be happy and there is no need to do something the other does not desire, but what the situation requires to have a happy marriage. Trust in yourselves, you do not play with your marriage, your children, with your happiness because you have the qualities necessary to have a happy marriage and happy children and to surpass all the difficulties that appear.

1861. The qualities of the wife make the husband happy.

1862. The qualities of parents make children happy.

1863. Each of us needs to discover all the qualities and to grow them as much as possible in order to increase the chances of meeting more favorable opportunities.

1864. A balanced life is due to the fact that a man has several qualities that have made life balanced.

1865. A balanced life contributes very much to the development of qualities.

1866. Co-development helps develop the necessary qualities for more effective co operations.

1867. Co-development helps shape and develop certain qualities that help in the formation and maintenance of a happy marriage.

1868. Co-development helps shape and develop qualities that help shape and develop true friendships.

1869. The Internet helps us develop qualities of interrelationship. Use it. Good luck.

1870. The more qualities we have the more chances we have to achieve consensus when it is necessary to obtain it.

1871. Achieving consensus helps us develop our qualities as negotiators.

1872. The one who also has the qualities to motivate others to act with efficiency can produce more personal goals.

1873. We can make our life more beautiful and if we have more qualities.

1874. If we have flaws and we do not have the qualities needed in what we do we will have failures.

1875. Each of us needs to discover all the qualities and to develop them as much as possible for the chance to achieve a true marriage.

1876. For as long as we live it is better to try to have relations of friendship with special people who have many successes, many qualities, many positive and effective behaviors in order to learn from them as much as we can. This rule, this principle helps us achieve more easily and with greater chances our personal goals.

1877. In life we have many more chances to meet favorable situations if we are friends with as many people as we can who have had successes, who have qualities, skills, effective behaviors, creative qualities, which are well documented in areas that concern us all.

1878. Many of us have the qualities and skills necessary to be educated and to grow properly, but unfortunately we do not spend time on this and we are making a big, a very big mistake which we will later regret in vain. Be attentive and success to those people who can prevent this mistake.

1879. Participating in social events helps us develop our necessary qualities for maintaining an efficient co-development.

1880. Forming, developing and using more and more qualities helps us prevent the situation of reaching despair.

1881. The more qualities we have and use effectively, the more chances we have not to reach the situation of despair.

1882. The activity of voluntarism can help us a lot in forming and developing our qualities.

1883. Each of us needs to find all the qualities we have and develop them as much as possible in order to increase our chances of maintaining mature love.

1884. Participating in social actions helps us develop our ability and necessary qualities for cooperation.

1885. The more qualities we have to use in achieving personal objectives the more trust we have in a better future.

1886. It is necessary that one of our objectives is the development of the necessary qualities for achieving our goals.

1887. The more qualities we have the more efficient our co operations are.

1888. Creative attitudes, qualities and capacities must be rewarded.

1889. Humanist thinking helps us a lot to form and develop humanist qualities.

1890. Each of us needs to discover all his qualities and develop them as much as possible for our big chance to maintain a happy marriage.

1891. Even if we reach the situation of despair we can very easily get rid of it most of the times because life was given to us to live it with the goods and bads, for we have the qualities necessary but we have to use them effectively.

1892. Those who are capable of self control in stressful situations have the qualities necessary to maintain true friends.

1893. A trust worthy man has more qualities.

1894. A man willing to try new ways has many creative qualities.

1895. Sportive events help maintain health, help develop more qualities and prevent more negative actions, a fact that is necessary to be supported and encouraged.

1896. Many of us can perform incredible deeds but we do not, not because we do not have the knowledge and qualities necessary to do them, but because we do not trust ourselves, our forces and some of us because we are not sufficiently motivated.

1897. By developing new abilities, new attitudes and new qualities we will increase our chances very much to achieve personal goals.

1898. The more qualities we have the more chances we have to meet more choices that we can make.

1899. People who inspire trust have more qualities.

1900. The majority of those who easily make true friends also have more qualities among which human qualities can be found.

1901. The size and quality of experience is not only given by a life's duration but also by the intensity with which it has been lived, how much time was the work day by day, the area one has worked in, what one has worked, the qualities, and abilities, aptitudes and attitudes that man has, etc.

1902. Co-development develops our social qualities.

1903. Those who know that discipline is one of the greatest qualities must be promoted.

1904. Those who know that discipline is one of the greatest qualities must be supported.

1905. Most of those involved in several projects also have creative qualities.

1906. People who have had successes know how to recognize both their qualities and defects very well.

1907. People who have humane social behaviors are engines of development of human qualities.

1908. Feminine qualities make men happy.

1909. Humanist scientific knowledge, human living experience, stored in books, on the Internet, in the media, human qualities allow the achievement of an incredibly high number of happy marriages, but, unfortunately, many people do not give the time and the attention necessary to achieving and maintaining a happy marriage.

1910. Some qualities create other qualities.

1911. A man with many qualities is highly appreciated.

1912. The more qualities a man has the more chances to has of achieving true friendships.

1913. The more qualities a man has the more chances he has to meet more favorable situations.

1914. The more qualities a man has the more chances he has of achieving efficient co-developments.

1915. A woman with many qualities more easily finds the suited partner.

1916. Women need to unite, to stay together and to cooperate in order to create a better world, because they have the abilities, the aptitudes, the qualities and the strength necessary to succeed.

1917. Humanist economy develops our humanist qualities.

1918. Industriousness forms and develops qualities.

1919. The more a man has more qualities the more appreciated he will be.

1920. The more qualities a man has the more chances he has of achieving many greater or smaller successes.

1921. The more qualities a man has, the more chances he has of achieving his personal objectives.

1922. The more a man has more qualities the more chances he has to achieve efficient co operations.

1923. Those who are preoccupied with creating on optimal cooperation in a team have the qualities and a much greater potential and chances to achieve efficient co-developments.

1924. An honest woman through her honesty and her qualities maintains a happy marriage.

1925. The more qualities we have the more chances we have to be lucky.

1926. Orientation towards a future world develops our prospective qualities.

1927. Those who have no hopes, in order to create their hopes need to develop the necessary qualities to help them discover where, when and how they can find favorable situations.

1928. People who have not succeeded in achieving a happy marriage up to a certain date, in order to succeed they need to form and develop the necessary qualities to achieve and maintain a balanced love relationship.

1929. Most of those who have not succeeded in achieving a happy marriage, in order to succeed they need to form and develop all their qualities.

1930. Those who have high objectives in life have the necessary qualities to face states of being worried.

1931. People who have the ability to take rapid quality decisions have many creative qualities.

1932. Persons with human social behaviors have more qualities to achieve efficient global co operations.

1933. Constructive thinking makes us have zero tolerance towards inequalities.

1934. The necessary qualities to achieve our personal goals can be formed, developed, maintained and used also through the contribution of the formation, development, maintenance and usage of an objective behavior.

1935. Our qualities can be formed, developed, maintained and used also through the contribution of the formation, development, maintenance and usage of global thinking.

1936. Some intellectual qualities are sometimes seductive.

1937. In order to pursue and transform positive objectives into reality it is necessary to form and develop the ability to form, develop and maintain the necessary qualities to achieve personal goals.

1938. The more qualities a man has the more chances he has of achieving his personal objectives.

1939. The more a man has more qualities the more efficient he is.

1940. We need to permanently enjoy the qualities we have.

1941. Friendships help us develop certain qualities.

1942. With friends it is always necessary to see their qualities.

1943. With friends it is always necessary to show them the qualities that they have.

1944. Efficient friendships help us form certain qualities.

1945. Efficient friendships help us develop certain qualities that help us achieve our personal goals.

1946. True friendships develop the qualities of friends.

1947. We must develop our creative qualities.

1948. Creative qualities help us a lot to succeed in life.

1949. Creative qualities can be developed.

1950. Creative qualities must be appreciated.

1951. Creative qualities help us a lot to achieve happy marriages.

1952. Creative qualities help us a lot to attain our personal goals.

1953. We must permanently develop our creative qualities.

1954. We must permanently enhance the efficiency of using creative qualities.

1955. We must recognize the qualities in everyone.

1956. We must appreciate the qualities in everyone.

1957. We must primarily see in every person his qualities.

1958. Spouses must see the qualities first in each other.

1959. We each have more or fewer qualities.

1960. We must each develop our qualities.

1961. We must each use our qualities.

1962. We must each know our qualities.

1963. Knowing ourselves helps us a lot to develop our qualities.

1964. AGC mediations help us discover qualities.

1965. Qualities must be appreciated.

1966. Qualities must be rewarded.

1967. Qualities lead us to successes.

1968. Qualities help us achieve a happy marriage.

1969. Qualities help us achieve more successes.

1970. Qualities help us achieve more personal goals.

1971. Qualities help us achieve more performances.

1972. Qualities help us achieve more efficient co operations.

1973. Qualities help us achieve more pleasant surprises.

1974. Qualities help us achieve more true friendships.

1975. Qualities help us achieve a true love.

1976. Cherishing oneself helps us develop our qualities.

1977. Creativity helps us develop our qualities.

1978. Creativity helps us form new qualities.

1979. By developing their inner beauty, women also develop their qualities.

1980. The necessary qualities in achieving personal goals can be formed, developed, maintained and used also through the contribution of the formation, development, maintenance and usage of reserved behavior.

1981. The necessary qualities in achieving personal goals can be formed, developed, maintained and used also through the contribution of the formation, development, maintenance and usage of active behavior.

1982. A great capacity of using qualities helps us achieve more favorable situations.

1983. The necessary qualities in achieving personal goals can be formed, developed, maintained and used also through the contribution of the formation, development, maintenance and usage of flexible behavior.

1984. Qualities must be supported.

1985. Qualities must be encouraged.

1986. Qualities must be imitated.

1987. Qualities must be formed.

1988. Qualities must be developed.

1989. Qualities must be maintained.

1990. Qualities must be used.

1991. The necessary qualities in achieving personal goals can be formed, developed, maintained and used also through the contribution of the formation, development, maintenance and usage of cultivated behavior.

1992. A great capacity of using qualities helps us become more productive.

1993. A great capacity of using qualities helps us become more efficient.

1994. The necessary qualities in achieving personal goals can be formed, developed, maintained and used also through the contribution of the formation, development, maintenance and usage of stable behavior.

1995. The necessary qualities in achieving personal goals can be formed, developed, maintained and used also through the

contribution of the formation, development, maintenance and usage of voluble behavior.

1996. A great capacity of using qualities helps us become optimistic.

1997. The necessary qualities in achieving personal goals can be formed, developed, maintained and used also through the contribution of the formation, development, maintenance and usage of systematic behavior.

1998. A great capacity of using qualities must be maintained.

1999. The necessary qualities in achieving personal goals can be formed, developed, maintained and used also through the contribution of the formation, development, maintenance and usage of good listener behavior.

2000. A great capacity of using qualities helps us achieve more pleasant surprises.

2001. A great capacity of using qualities helps us become loving.

2002. The necessary qualities in achieving personal goals can be formed, developed, maintained and used also through the contribution of the formation, development, maintenance and usage of conscientious behavior.

2003. The necessary qualities in achieving personal goals can be formed, developed, maintained and used also through the contribution of the formation, development, maintenance and usage of imaginative behavior.

2004. The necessary qualities in achieving personal goals can be formed, developed, maintained and used also through the contribution of the formation, development, maintenance and usage of reasonable behavior.

2005. The necessary qualities in achieving personal goals can be formed, developed, maintained and used also through the contribution of the formation, development, maintenance and usage of content behavior.

2006. A great capacity of using qualities helps us maintain our enthusiasm.

2007. A great capacity of using qualities helps us maintain our productivity.

2008. The necessary qualities in achieving personal goals can be formed, developed, maintained and used also through the contribution of the formation, development, maintenance and usage of penetrating behavior.

2009. The necessary qualities in achieving personal goals can be formed, developed, maintained and used also through the contribution of the formation, development, maintenance and usage of friendly behavior.

2010. A great capacity of using qualities helps us maintain our tolerance.

2011. The necessary qualities in achieving personal goals can be formed, developed, maintained and used also through the contribution of the formation, development, maintenance and usage of working behavior.

2012. The necessary qualities in achieving personal goals can be formed, developed, maintained and used also through the contribution of the formation, development, maintenance and usage of expansive behavior.

2013. The necessary qualities in achieving personal goals can be formed, developed, maintained and used also through the contribution of the formation, development, maintenance and usage of productive behavior.

2014. The necessary qualities in achieving personal goals can be formed, developed, maintained and used also through the contribution of the formation, development, maintenance and usage of adaptable behavior.

2015. The necessary qualities in achieving personal goals can be formed, developed, maintained and used also through the contribution of the formation, development, maintenance and usage of calm behavior.

2016. The necessary qualities in achieving personal goals can be formed, developed,

maintained and used also through the contribution of the formation, development, maintenance and usage of optimistic behavior.

2017. A great capacity of using qualities helps us become more loving.

2018. A great capacity of using qualities helps us achieve more true friendships.

2019. The necessary qualities in achieving personal goals can be formed, developed, maintained and used also through the contribution of the formation, development, maintenance and usage of brave behavior.

2020. A great capacity of using qualities helps us maintain our happiness.

2021. The necessary qualities in achieving personal goals can be formed, developed, maintained and used also through the contribution of the formation, development, maintenance and usage of astute behavior.

2022. A great capacity of using qualities helps us become cautious.

2023. A great capacity of using qualities helps us become tolerant.

2024. The necessary qualities in achieving personal goals can be formed, developed, maintained and used also through the contribution of the formation, development, maintenance and usage of fighting behavior.

2025. The necessary qualities in achieving personal goals can be formed, developed, maintained and used also through the contribution of the formation, development, maintenance and usage of balanced behavior.

2026. A great capacity of using qualities must be appreciated.

2027. The necessary qualities in achieving personal goals can be formed, developed, maintained and used also through the contribution of the formation, development, maintenance and usage of intellectual behavior.

2028. A great capacity of using qualities helps us maintain our efficiency.

2029. A great capacity of using qualities helps us become more enthusiastic.

2030. The necessary qualities in achieving personal goals can be formed, developed, maintained and used also through the contribution of the formation, development, maintenance and usage of the loyal behavior.

2031. A great capacity of using qualities must be used.

2032. The necessary qualities in achieving personal goals can be formed, developed, maintained and used also through the contribution of the formation, development, maintenance and usage of cheerful behavior.

2033. A great capacity of using qualities helps us maintain our way of being loved.

2034. A great capacity of using qualities helps us achieve more personal goals.

2035. The necessary qualities in achieving personal goals can be formed, developed, maintained and used also through the contribution of the formation, development,

maintenance and usage of efficient behavior.

2036. A great capacity of using qualities helps us achieve more performances.

2037. The necessary qualities in achieving personal goals can be formed, developed, maintained and used also through the contribution of the formation, development, maintenance and usage of independent behavior.

2038. The necessary qualities in achieving personal goals can be formed, developed, maintained and used also through the contribution of the formation, development, maintenance and usage of meticulous behavior.

2039. The necessary qualities in achieving personal goals can be formed, developed, maintained and used also through the contribution of the formation, development, maintenance and usage of peacemaking behavior.

2040. The necessary qualities in achieving personal goals can be formed, developed, maintained and used also through the

contribution of the formation, development, maintenance and usage of unpretentious behavior.

2041. The necessary qualities in achieving personal goals can be formed, developed, maintained and used also through the contribution of the formation, development, maintenance and usage of continuous self perfecting behavior.

2042. The necessary qualities in achieving personal goals can be formed, developed, maintained and used also through the contribution of the formation, development, maintenance and usage of convincing behavior.

2043. A great capacity of using qualities helps us maintain our way of being understanding.

2044. A great capacity of using qualities must be a model.

2045. The necessary qualities in achieving personal goals can be formed, developed, maintained and used also through the contribution of the formation, development, maintenance and usage of docile behavior.

2046. The necessary qualities in achieving personal goals can be formed, developed, maintained and used also through the contribution of the formation, development, maintenance and usage of trained behavior.

2047. A great capacity of using qualities helps us become understanding.

2048. A great capacity of using qualities helps us become more preventive.

2049. The necessary qualities in achieving personal goals can be formed, developed, maintained and used also through the contribution of the formation, development, maintenance and usage of positive behavior.

2050. The necessary qualities in achieving personal goals can be formed, developed, maintained and used also through the contribution of the formation, development, maintenance and usage of a behavior of continuously efficiently using our time.

2051. The necessary qualities in achieving personal goals can be formed, developed, maintained and used also through the

contribution of the formation, development, maintenance and usage of pleasant behavior.

2052. The necessary qualities in achieving personal goals can be formed, developed, maintained and used also through the contribution of the formation, development, maintenance and usage of spontaneous behavior.

2053. The necessary qualities in achieving personal goals can be formed, developed, maintained and used also through the contribution of the formation, development, maintenance and usage of confident behavior.

2054. The necessary qualities in achieving personal goals can be formed, developed, maintained and used also through the contribution of the formation, development, maintenance and usage of sensitive behavior.

2055. The necessary qualities in achieving personal goals can be formed, developed, maintained and used also through the contribution of the formation, development,

maintenance and usage of realistic behavior.

2056. A great capacity of using qualities helps us become loved.

2057. A great capacity of using qualities helps us become happier.

2058. The necessary qualities in achieving personal goals can be formed, developed, maintained and used also through the contribution of the formation, development, maintenance and usage of demanding behavior.

2059. A great capacity of using qualities helps us become wise.

2060. The necessary qualities in achieving personal goals can be formed, developed, maintained and used also through the contribution of the formation, development, maintenance and usage of tenacious behavior.

2061. The necessary qualities in achieving personal goals can be formed, developed, maintained and used also through the

contribution of the formation, development, maintenance and usage of joyful behavior.

2062. The necessary qualities in achieving personal goals can be formed, developed, maintained and used also through the contribution of the formation, development, maintenance and usage of firm behavior.

2063. A great capacity of using qualities helps us become efficient.

2064. A great capacity of using qualities must be rewarded.

2065. A great capacity of using qualities helps us maintain our wisdom.

2066. The necessary qualities in achieving personal goals can be formed, developed, maintained and used also through the contribution of the formation, development, maintenance and usage of a behavior of being inclined towards research.

2067. A great capacity of using qualities helps us become humane.

2068. The necessary qualities in achieving personal goals can be formed, developed,

maintained and used also through the contribution of the formation, development, maintenance and usage of continuous self-controlling behavior.

2069. A great capacity of using qualities helps us become more understanding.

2070. The necessary qualities in achieving personal goals can be formed, developed, maintained and used also through the contribution of the formation, development, maintenance and usage of capable behavior.

2071. A great capacity of using qualities must be supported.

2072. A great capacity of using qualities must be imitated.

2073. A great capacity of using qualities helps us maintain our way of being liked.

2074. The necessary qualities in achieving personal goals can be formed, developed, maintained and used also through the contribution of the formation, development, maintenance and usage of patient behavior.

2075. The necessary qualities in achieving personal goals can be formed, developed, maintained and used also through the contribution of the formation, development, maintenance and usage of daring behavior.

2076. A great capacity of using qualities helps us maintain our humanity.

2077. The necessary qualities in achieving personal goals can be formed, developed, maintained and used also through the contribution of the formation, development, maintenance and usage of charitable behavior.

2078. A great capacity of using qualities must be encouraged.

2079. The necessary qualities in achieving personal goals can be formed, developed, maintained and used also through the contribution of the formation, development, maintenance and usage of understanding behavior.

2080. The necessary qualities in achieving personal goals can be formed, developed, maintained and used also through the

contribution of the formation, development, maintenance and usage of funny behavior.

2081. A great capacity of using qualities helps us become more cautious.

2082. The necessary qualities in achieving personal goals can be formed, developed, maintained and used also through the contribution of the formation, development, maintenance and usage of loyal behavior.

2083. A great capacity of using qualities must be developed.

2084. The necessary qualities in achieving personal goals can be formed, developed, maintained and used also through the contribution of the formation, development, maintenance and usage of bold behavior.

2085. The necessary qualities in achieving personal goals can be formed, developed, maintained and used also through the contribution of the formation, development, maintenance and usage of rigorous behavior.

2086. A great capacity of using qualities helps us achieve more records.

2087. The necessary qualities in achieving personal goals can be formed, developed, maintained and used also through the contribution of the formation, development, maintenance and usage of sociable behavior.

2088. The necessary qualities in achieving personal goals can be formed, developed, maintained and used also through the contribution of the formation, development, maintenance and usage of leading behavior.

2089. The necessary qualities in achieving personal goals can be formed, developed, maintained and used also through the contribution of the formation, development, maintenance and usage of cautious behavior.

2090. A great capacity of using qualities helps us become practical.

2091. The necessary qualities in achieving personal goals can be formed, developed, maintained and used also through the contribution of the formation, development,

maintenance and usage of a behavior of being in a good mood.

2092. A great capacity of using qualities helps us achieve more efficient co operations.

2093. The necessary qualities in achieving personal goals can be formed, developed, maintained and used also through the contribution of the formation, development, maintenance and usage of ingenious behavior.

2094. The necessary qualities in achieving personal goals can be formed, developed, maintained and used also through the contribution of the formation, development, maintenance and usage of hardworking behavior.

2095. A great capacity of using qualities helps us achieve more favorable chances.

2096. The necessary qualities in achieving personal goals can be formed, developed, maintained and used also through the contribution of the formation, development, maintenance and usage of popular behavior.

2097. The necessary qualities in achieving personal goals can be formed, developed, maintained and used also through the contribution of the formation, development, maintenance and usage of enthusiastic behavior.

2098. The necessary qualities in achieving personal goals can be formed, developed, maintained and used also through the contribution of the formation, development, maintenance and usage of respectful behavior.

2099. The necessary qualities in achieving personal goals can be formed, developed, maintained and used also through the contribution of the formation, development, maintenance and usage of humane behavior.

2100. A great capacity of using qualities helps us maintain our way of being loving.

2101. A great capacity of using qualities helps us achieve more successes.

2102. The necessary qualities in achieving personal goals can be formed, developed, maintained and used also through the

contribution of the formation, development, maintenance and usage of spiritual behavior.

2103. The necessary qualities in achieving personal goals can be formed, developed, maintained and used also through the contribution of the formation, development, maintenance and usage of peaceful behavior.

2104. The necessary qualities in achieving personal goals can be formed, developed, maintained and used also through the contribution of the formation, development, maintenance and usage of charming behavior.

2105. The necessary qualities in achieving personal goals can be formed, developed, maintained and used also through the contribution of the formation, development, maintenance and usage of kind behavior.

2106. The necessary qualities in achieving personal goals can be formed, developed, maintained and used also through the contribution of the formation, development,

maintenance and usage of continuous self economizing behavior.

Woman

2107. The inner beauty of the woman creates many joys to those around her.

2108. The cuddling behavior of the woman seduces the man.

2109. The cuddling behavior of the woman contributes a lot to achieving a long lasting love.

2110. The cuddling behavior of the woman contributes a lot to maintaining a long lasting love.

2111. The cuddling behavior of the woman contributes a lot to achieving a happy love.

2112. Each woman has the need not to feel ignored.

2113. Each woman has the need to feel admired.

2114. Each woman has the need to feel accepted.

2115. Each woman needs that the man takes care of her.

2116. Each woman has the need to feel loved.

2117. Each woman has the need to be loved.

2118. Each woman has the need not to be criticized.

2119. Each woman has the need not to be ignored.

2120. Each woman has the need not to be disrespected.

2121. Each woman has the need not to be terrorized.

2122. Each woman has the need to feel like she is right.

2123. Each woman has the need not to be neglected.

2124. Each woman has the need to be understood.

2125. Each woman has the need not to feel the lack of support.

2126. Each woman needs understanding from the man.

2127. Each woman has the need to feel like he cares about her.

2128. Each woman has the need to feel approved.

2129. Each woman has the need to feel like he cares about her feelings.

2130. Each woman has the need not to feel the lack of safety.

2131. Each woman has the need to feel that her need to obtain information is respected.

2132. Each woman has the need to feel taken into account.

2133. Each woman has the need to feel that he is listening.

2134. Each woman has the need to be understood why she is in a bad mood.

2135. Each woman has the need not to feel condemned.

2136. Each woman has the need not to be pulled down.

2137. Each woman has the need not to feel the lack of protection.

2138. Each woman has the need to feel respected.

2139. Each woman has the need not to be unappreciated.

2140. Each woman has the need not to feel the lack of affection.

Women

2141. The more we meet more men or women the better chances we have to meet the right partner for life. An ideal place to meet them is the Internet being aware of the advantages, disadvantages and risks that it offers. Good luck! Persevere because I am sure you will be able to find the right partner for life. Good luck.

2142. Most women and men want a happy marriage, but unfortunately they do too little, they give too little time, too little attention to achieve and to maintain it. If, instead, they do all that is necessary to achieve and maintain a happy marriage, they will surely make it. We wish you success confident that you will be able to build and maintain a happy marriage. Good luck again.

2143. A man must always appreciate the qualities of women.

2144. Love for the vast majority of women is particularly important. Given this fact in having a relationship of true love, unfortunately, many facts are unacceptable.

2145. True love for women is a very important need.

2146. In many cases both women and men go quickly from a type of friendly intimacy to love.

2147. Sometimes some women seeking love may be devoid of scruples.

2148. There are many situations in which women have greater efficiency than men.

2149. Sometimes there are certain situations in which women do what men can do.

2150. Men need to respect women for their outstanding positive facts.

2151. Women should not feel that men are complexing them.

2152. Men without women can not be fully happy again.

2153. Women ensure true marital happiness.

2154. Women who are aggressive against their family members may change their aggressive behavior to be a non-aggressive behavior in any family situation.

2155. Good humor can be maintained through a balanced life, a proper diet, education, intellectual exercises, psychical balance, perseverance, women, physical exercises, a value system in which we believe in and that we respect, positive activities, dynamism, social relations, friends, mature love, a happy marriage, etc.

2156. Women are mostly abused in family violence.

2157. The more men or women we meet from case to case, the better chances we have to meet the right life partner. An ideal place to meet him/her is the Internet, taking into account the advantages, disadvantages and risks that it offers us. Good luck. Persevere as I am sure you will be able to find the right partner for life. Good luck.

2158. Most women and men are looking for a happy marriage, but unfortunately they do too little, give too little time, too little attention to that and to achieving and maintaining it. If on the contrary, they will do what is necessary to achieve and maintain a happy marriage, they will surely achieve it. I wish you success with the confidence that you will be able to achieve and maintain a happy marriage. Good luck again.

2159. Men who have relationships with women with higher incomes than them must not feel like that is a complex.

2160. It is absolutely normal that some women or many women earn more than men.

2161. Men must respect women who earn more than they do.

2162. Men need to be glad that women manage to have larger incomes than they do, because they have nothing to lose and should not have prejudices.

2163. Men must not have prejudices towards women.

2164. Men need to support and sustain women in everything positive that they do without a trace of prejudice.

2165. The discrimination of men towards women, their where it exists, must disappear as soon as possible.

2166. The co-development of men and women stop and prevent discriminations.

2167. The co-development of men and women is in both men and women's advantage.

2168. The co-development of men and women makes both men and women a lot happier.

2169. The co-development of men and women does them good, helps them achieve happy marriages.

2170. The co-development of women and men is a necessity for society.

2171. Magnanimity can be met both in women and men regardless of their age.

Biography

Gheorghe Cornel Ardelean was born on March 11.1954 in place Macea, Arad Country Romania Graduate of Economic University, Craiova Romania

1979-1989 Economist and Chief Economist and sales Department

In 1990-founding member of the first Parliament of Romania after the Revolution of 1989 in PCNU (Provisional Council of National Unity)

1992 - Independent candidate for deputy in the Romanian Parliament, Chamber of Deputies

1992-1996 Advisor to the Arad Country Council as an independent adviser

1992-1996 President of the Commission trade, tourism, services advise Arad Country Council

1990-2002 Director, manager of private companies wholesale

1980 - Philosopher and author books.

1980 He published 118 books, articles in publications, of which 50 English books and 68 books in Romanian

In 2009 - Member and Coordinator of Department programs, projects and activities of the non-profit. International Organisation Cornel Gheorghe Ardelean (OIAGC)

As a thought on long-term, positive, constructive, open, creative, humanistic, etc. It has a great ability to create so many positive ideas and solutions, constructive, humanist, creative, helpful people to achieve what they want. Thinking and ideas sustain and promote the rights of children, women, all people in the world, positive thinking and ideas, constructive, humanistic, tolerante, progressive, understanding and peace between peoples and nations.

www.ingramcontent.com/pod-product-compliance
Lightning Source LLC
Chambersburg PA
CBHW062128280526
45788CB00001B/93